THE ALLERGY-FREE
COOKBOOK

THE ALLERGY-FREE COOKBOOK

OVER 50 DELICIOUS AND HEALTHY RECIPES FOR ALLERGY SUFFERERS

CONTRIBUTING EDITOR:
MAGGIE PANNELL

LORENZ BOOKS

First published in 1999 by Lorenz Books

LORENZ BOOKS are available for bulk purchase for sales promotion
and for premium use. For details, write or call the sales director, Lorenz Books
27 West 20th Street, New York, NY 10011; (800) 354-9657

ISBN 0 7548 0182 9

Publisher: Joanna Lorenz
Executive Editor: Linda Fraser
Designer: Carole Perks
Reader: Marion Wilson
Production Controller: Joanna King
Photographers: Karl Adamson, Nicki Dowey, Michelle Garrett, Amanda Heywood
and William Lingwood (Pictures on pp9 and 12 Tony Stone Images)
Recipes: Angela Boggiano, Jacqueline Clarke, Carole Clements, Joanna Farrow, Christine France,
Shirley Gill, Christine Ingram, Kathy Mann, Lesley Mackley, Maggie Mayhew, Sallie Morris, Jennie
Shapter, Kate Whiteman, Elizabeth Wolf-Cohen and Jeni Wright

Printed and bound in Singapore

1 3 5 7 9 10 8 6 4 2

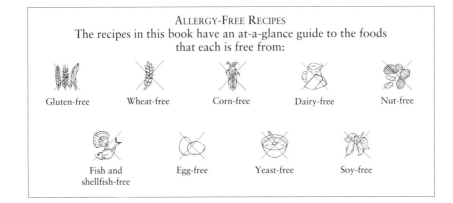

ALLERGY-FREE RECIPES
The recipes in this book have an at-a-glance guide to the foods
that each is free from:

Gluten-free   Wheat-free   Corn-free   Dairy-free   Nut-free

Fish and   Egg-free   Yeast-free   Soy-free
shellfish-free

CONTENTS

Introduction 6
The Healthy Diet 8
Cereal Foods 10
Milk and Other Dairy Products 12
Other Problem Foods 14
What about Additives? 16
Testing for Food Allergy 18
Allergy-free Eating 20
Cooking for Children 21

Soups, Appetizers and Salads 22

Meat and Poultry 40

Fish and Shellfish 56

Vegetables and Vegetarian Dishes 68

Desserts and Baked Goods 82

Information File 95

Index 96

INTRODUCTION

If you've ever developed a bad migraine or an irritating skin rash, or perhaps a digestive problem or a stuffy nose that doesn't then become a cold, it may be that the condition was caused not by illness but by something to which you are allergic or sensitive. Depending on the severity of the symptoms, this may be either a mild, short-term nuisance or a more serious condition, such as asthma or coeliac disease. It's not known just how common "allergies" are. Potential causes are numerous and can be difficult to identify.

The aim of this chapter is to help you discover if something that you're eating or drinking could be the cause of your symptoms. Once you've tracked down the cause of the problem, this book has helpful advice on how to adapt your diet to be nutritionally balanced while excluding anything to which you're sensitive. By investigating your symptoms and excluding suspect foods from your diet, you can discover the culprit(s) causing the reaction and use these delicious and easily prepared recipes to help you enjoy a healthy, allergy-free life.

WHAT IS AN ALLERGY?

An allergy is a reaction that occurs when the body's immune (defense) system overreacts to a normally harmless substance, causing irritation, disability and sometimes even fatality. A substance that causes an allergy is called an allergen and can be anything in the environment—whether it's something ingested, inhaled or that touches the skin—that causes an adverse reaction. Among the most commonly found allergens are pollen, dust mites, pet hair, insect stings, chemicals or food or drink.

Our immune system usually protects us from harmful foreign invaders, such as viruses and bacteria, that might otherwise cause illness. In the allergic person, however, the system believes that the allergen is damaging and reacts to it accordingly. A special type of antibody, called IgE (immunoglobulin E), is produced to fend off the threatening substance, triggering the release of chemicals, such as histamine. These cause the unpleasant symptoms, such as rashes, inflammation or wheezing, that are often associated with an allergic reaction.

HOW COMMON ARE ALLERGIES?

It is not known just how common allergies are, as the potential causes are numerous and can be difficult to identify. It is not even known exactly how many people react badly to certain substances, since many cases are mild enough to be undetected or may be misdiagnosed: an individual's desire to label a condition can lead them to a mistaken conclusion about a cause and its effect.

It has been suggested that as many as 25 percent of the population will suffer from an intolerance at some point in their lives. Asthma, eczema and hay fever, for example, are very common and appear to be on the increase. This may be a consequence of a number of factors, including increased air pollution, greater use of chemicals, modern living conditions and more stressful lifestyles.

Surprisingly, the onset of an allergy or intolerance can occur at any age and the substance may be something that has previously been tolerated. Equally, sensitivity can be outgrown, and troublesome symptoms completely disappear.

THE DIFFERENCE BETWEEN ALLERGY, INTOLERANCE AND SENSITIVITY

Strictly speaking, the word allergy should only be used to describe a specific response caused by an over-reaction of the immune system. An intolerance, however, is a broader term describing any unpleasant reaction to an offending substance. Hypersensitivity can be used as a general description

Above: Chocolate and drinks, such as tea, coffee and cola, contain caffeine.

Above: A migraine can be caused by eating chocolate or cheese, or by drinking red wine.

SYMPTOMS THAT MAY SUGGEST AN ALLERGY OR INTOLERANCE

Symptoms of hypersensitivity are numerous but common reactions typically include:

- sneezing and a constant runny nose (perennial rhinitis)
- wheezing, coughing and shortness of breath (asthma)
- itchy rashes (nettle-like urticaria) and dry, flaky skin (eczema)
- sinus problems
- headaches or migraine
- lethargy
- loss of concentration
- flu-like aches and pains
- an uncomfortable bloated feeling
- diarrhea
- vomiting
- flatulence

covering both allergy and intolerance, although none of these should be confused with food aversion, which has psychological roots.

There are many different causes of food intolerance, which may be linked to the behavior of various enzymes or bacteria in the body. Lactose (milk sugar) intolerance, for example, is not an allergic reaction but occurs because a person has insufficient lactase enzyme, which is needed for the digestion of lactose.

There are also a number of substances in food that can cause a reaction in some people. Caffeine in tea, coffee, chocolate and cola, for instance, can bring on palpitations and restless behavior, while amines found in red wine, chocolate and cheese can trigger a migraine. These are not true allergic reactions, although the term allergy is frequently loosely used for describing all sorts of food intolerance.

Right: Pet hair may cause an allergic reaction that results in irritation to the eyes, nose and skin and difficulty in breathing.

NON-FOOD ALLERGENS

Discover the cause of your allergy, then take action to avoid the substance or to minimize your exposure to it. Could one of these allergens be to blame?

Dust mites—Modern homes often have carpets, double glazing, central heating and poor ventilation, providing ideal conditions for dust mites to thrive. You should vacuum regularly, wet-wipe surfaces, consider wood and linoleum flooring rather than carpets, and blinds rather than curtains. Open windows as often as possible.

Insect (bee and wasp) stings—These may cause pain and swelling and occasionally anaphylactic shock.

Jewelry—Metal allergy (especially to nickel) can cause skin irritation.

Medicines—Aspirin and penicillin and other antibiotics can cause an allergic reaction.

Pets—Fur and feathers may be responsible for allergic rhinitis, asthma and eczema.

Pollen—Hay fever is a common allergy. It causes itchy eyes, sneezing and a blocked nose, especially when the sufferer ventures outdoors, and particularly in early summer. To reduce the symptoms, it is best to avoid over-exposure by closing windows and wearing sunglasses.

Toiletries and cosmetics—Perfumed products can be a problem so try changing to a pure formulation or using non-allergenic makeup.

Above: Beauty preparations and soaps with non-allergenic formulas are now widely available and popular for their purity.

THE HEALTHY DIET

Before investigating whether your symptoms could be caused by an allergy or intolerance to any particular food, it is important first of all to establish that you are eating healthily. A poor diet could be the reason for certain conditions, which may disappear once your diet is improved. So let's take a closer look at what constitutes a healthy diet. We all know that variety and balance are important, but how do you put that theory into practice? Healthy eating is one of the most important ways in which we can look after our health. It doesn't mean banning foods on the grounds that they're high in fat, sugar or salt. It means choosing a wide variety of foods to obtain the balance of nutrients that are needed for the development and maintenance of a healthy body.

HOW TO CHOOSE A HEALTHY BALANCE

Bread, cereals and potatoes—These are the starchy carbohydrate foods that provide sustained energy as well as important vitamins and minerals and some protein. Whole-grain types, such as whole-wheat bread and brown rice, and potatoes in their skins, are a particularly good source of dietary fiber, which reduces the risk of intestinal disorders. This group of foods also includes pasta, white rice, breakfast cereals, oats, couscous, polenta, beans, lentils and starchy vegetables, such as yams and plantains. Carbohydrates should form the main part of your meals. They are not fattening or high in calories provided you don't add much fat or sugar when cooking or serving them.

Above: Bread and vegetables, such as plantains and potatoes, are rich in carbohydrate.

Fruits and vegetables—These foods are packed with valuable minerals and the antioxidant vitamins, beta carotene (a form of vitamin A) and vitamins C and E. Antioxidant vitamins are believed to help protect the body against free radicals, which can lead to degenerative diseases, such as heart disease and some cancers. Fruits and vegetables are also low in fat and calories and contain a type of fiber that may help to reduce blood cholesterol. With such a wide choice available, eating the recommended "five a day" is easy and produce doesn't always have to be fresh. Frozen, dried and canned fruits and vegetables may be more convenient and help to add variety.

Dairy foods—This group of foods, which includes milk, cheese and yogurt, helps provide protein and B group vitamins and is an excellent source of calcium, which is needed for strong bones and normal blood clotting. However, dairy foods can be high in saturated fat, so only eat moderate amounts. Choose skim or

HOW TO BOOST YOUR FRUIT AND VEGETABLE INTAKE

- Slice fruit, such as bananas or peaches, onto your breakfast cereal.
- Keep the fruit bowl well stocked to provide healthy snacks.
- Keep packages of dried fruits, such as apricots and prunes, on hand for popping into lunch boxes.

- Top baked potatoes with chili beans, ratatouille or corn to make a satisfying lunch.
- Serve raw vegetable crudités with a dip for an appetizer.
- Stir-fry vegetables with rice or noodles to make a quick meal.

- Pack sandwiches generously with crisp salad ingredients.
- Boost soups, stews, casseroles, homemade burgers and pasta sauces with extra vegetables.
- Make fresh fruit salads and dried fruit compotes for quick desserts.

Above: Chicken and meat are major sources of protein, but choose lean, skinless cuts.

Above: The protein and fatty acids found in oily fish are essential to a healthy diet.

low-fat milk and other low-fat dairy foods, which provide just as much calcium as whole varieties.

Meat, fish and other protein foods—These are major sources of vitamins and minerals in our diet (red meat especially provides iron and Vitamin B$_{12}$), but they don't need to be eaten in large amounts. Choose lean meat, poultry and game and opt for healthy, low-fat cooking methods, such as grilling, steaming and stir-frying. It is a good idea to eat fish at least twice a week, especially oily varieties, such as herring, sardines, mackerel, salmon and tuna, because they contain Omega-3 fatty acids, which are thought to help reduce the risk of heart disease. Other foods in this group, such as peas, beans, lentils, nuts, eggs, tempeh and soy products, provide alternative protein sources for vegetarians and people on special diets.

Occasional foods—Cookies, cakes, chips, French fries, pies, pastries, puddings, ice cream, chocolate, candy,

fats, salad dressings and soft drinks all tend to be high in fat and/or sugar (and therefore high in calories) and they are less nourishing than other foods. These foods should be eaten in moderation; too much of them can lead to weight gain and dental problems, especially if they are eaten between meals or as substitutes for healthier choices. Alcohol, too, should be drunk in moderation. It is a rich source of calories, but has very little nutrient value.

ORGANIC FOODS
These are foods that have been produced without the use of chemical pesticides and fertilizers, or genetically modified materials. The strict rules governing all products sold as organic are guaranteed by certification bodies.

Organic foods cost more to produce and are therefore more expensive than other foods, but growing public demand has led to much greater availability, which should in time make their price more competitive. The range of organic foods now available includes a variety of fresh produce, as well as meat, dairy and cereal foods, preserves, chocolate, wine and beer.

> ## THE ADVANTAGES OF A HEALTHY WHOLE-FOOD DIET
> ● Your weight will take care of itself without having to diet or count calories.
> ● There's less chance of developing degenerative diseases, such as heart disease, some cancers, bowel disorders and osteoporosis.
> ● You will have more energy and feel and look more vibrant.
> ● Tooth decay and gum disease will be less of a problem.

Left: Besides fresh fruits and vegetables, organic produce includes wine and beer as well as bread and cheese.

CEREAL FOODS

Because people are more likely to experience sensitivity to foods that they eat frequently, those who are sensitive to cereals make up one of the most common food intolerance groups. There are two different cereal-related allergies that can arise. The first is an extreme intolerance to gluten (the protein found in wheat, rye, barley and oats), which causes coeliac disease, a condition that is medically well recognized and affects between 1 in 1,000–1,500 people. The second is an intolerance to a single cereal, such as wheat (most common in Western countries), corn (most common in North America, where corn products are widely eaten), and rice (although this is very rare). People who have intolerance to one cereal can usually eat other cereals without any adverse affects.

COELIAC DISEASE

Coeliac (pronounced see-lee-ack) disease is caused when the protein complex gluten irritates and damages the lining of the small intestine. The consequence is that food is poorly absorbed and causes malnutrition.

Gluten protein is found in wheat and is similar to the proteins that are found in rye, barley and oats, which means that all these cereals have to be avoided. Sometimes oats may be tolerated because they contain less gluten.

The condition may first become apparent in a small child, when weaning foods are first introduced, but it is more common for the disease to be diagnosed in adulthood. The cause is unknown but the condition is inherited and can therefore run in families.

Once coeliac disease has been diagnosed, it is necessary to follow a gluten-free diet for life. Unlike some other food intolerances, people cannot outgrow this condition but, by avoiding gluten, can enjoy a full and healthy life.

THE SYMPTOMS OF COELIAC DISEASE

Typically, the symptoms of coeliac disease include:
- diarrhea
- vomiting
- weight loss
- anemia
- extreme tiredness
- recurrent mouth ulcers

An infant with coeliac disease will fail to grow and thrive when cereals that contain gluten are introduced to its diet. He or she will be miserable and lethargic with a poor appetite, pass pale, bulky and soft stools, and develop a potbelly. It is important that the condition is diagnosed early in order to prevent severe malnutrition and poor health, so seek medical advice if you are concerned.

WHEAT ALLERGY

If you have an intolerance or allergy to wheat or other cereals, the symptoms may be less serious than for coeliac disease but can still cause misery and discomfort. Many of these symptoms may have another cause so it is impossible to draw immediate conclusions.

You may suffer, for example, from any or all of the following:
- persistent digestive upsets
- fatigue
- joint pain
- asthma
- rhinitis
- skin complaints

FOOD LABELING

The words "gluten-free" appear on products purported to be suitable for people with a gluten intolerance. However, it is worth checking the ingredients list for less obvious gluten sources: binder; cereal protein; corn starch; edible starch, food starch or modified starch; rusk; thickener or vegetable protein.

DIAGNOSIS

Because the symptoms of coeliac disease are both apparent and specific, it is likely to be quickly diagnosed. Your doctor may suspect the condition if you are suffering from its typical symptoms and he or she will probably refer you to a hospital outpatients' department for an intestinal biopsy, which is performed under mild sedation. This will confirm whether or not the condition is present. Once coeliac disease has been diagnosed, you can adjust your diet to dispel the symptoms. However, sufferers from coeliac disease are more likely to be also intolerant of other foods, such as lactose and soy, so further investigation may be necessary.

If you are suffering from a wheat or other cereal intolerance, with vaguer and more general symptoms, it may take longer to identify the cause of your problem. The culprit(s) can usually only be accurately discovered by following an exclusion and challenge diet.

OTHER CONDITIONS RELATED TO GLUTEN INTOLERANCE

Those suffering from the rare skin disorder *dermatitis herpetiformis* can be helped by following a gluten-free diet. There are several other conditions that may be alleviated, but more medical research is needed to support this theory. These conditions include:
- multiple sclerosis
- rheumatoid arthritis
- Crohn's disease

Above: Some common foods containing wheat include bread, cake, pasta, wheat cereals, crackers and processed soups.

Above: Barley, rye and oats can be eaten by people with a wheat intolerance but not by those with a gluten intolerance.

Above: Foods that should be avoided if you have an intolerance to corn include cornflakes, corn oil, tortillas and popcorn.

WHAT FOODS DO YOU NEED TO AVOID?

Gluten intolerance—Unfortunately wheat and cereals make up a large part of the diet, so if coeliac disease is diagnosed, it means making considerable changes. As well as cutting out wheat-based foods, such as bread, flour, pasta, semolina, couscous, bulgur and certain breakfast cereals, wheat is also contained in processed foods, such as cakes, cookies, crackers, pastries, puddings, soups, sauces, gravy, stuffing mixes and sausages. You will also need to avoid rye and barley (including malted bedtime drinks) and possibly oats, depending on the nature of your intolerance. However, never start a gluten-free diet without first consulting your doctor.

Wheat intolerance—If only wheat is suspected, you will need to exclude all sources of wheat, wheat starch and wheat protein (gluten) from your diet. However, you will still be able to enjoy other cereals, such as barley, rye and oats. This type of intolerance may not be a lifelong condition. Sometimes small amounts of wheat can gradually be reintroduced without causing further problems.

Corn (maize) intolerance—Corn does not contain any gluten. However, it can still cause problems, especially if it is eaten frequently. Avoid cornflakes and other corn cereals, polenta, corn oil, tortilla, corn snacks, corn, popcorn, and cornstarch. Check the ingredient labels on manufactured foods for cornstarch, cornmeal and corn oil.

ALTERNATIVE CEREAL FOODS

A restricted diet can seem rather daunting initially, especially if it means giving up a lot of the foods that have previously been enjoyed. However, there are plenty of alternative products available from supermarkets and health food stores.

Changing to a gluten-free diet takes adjustment, but your meals can still be

Above: Gluten-free alternatives to wheat include chick-peas, rice, buckwheat, polenta, soy foods, potato flour and tapioca.

interesting and nutritionally balanced. Specially produced gluten-free flour, as well as potato flour, arrowroot, cornstarch, buckwheat flour, soy flour, ground rice or chickpea flour (besan) are all good substitutes for wheat flour. Cooked and puréed starchy vegetables can often be used for thickening soups and sauces.

There is a wide range of commercially made gluten-free foods, such as breads, cakes, cookies, pasta, muesli, crackers and rusks, some of which may be available by prescription. Gluten-free products may include wheat starch, so be aware if you are sensitive to wheat rather than gluten. It is advisable to check ingredient labels on manufactured foods.

ENSURING A HEALTHY DIET

You can enjoy all meat, fish and poultry other than products prepared in batter, bread crumbs or certain sauces. Eat plenty of fresh produce and a variety of other cereal products to ensure that your diet isn't lacking in nutrients and dietary fiber. Dairy products and eggs provide a good source of nourishment as long as there isn't a further intolerance evident. A nutritionist will be able to offer valuable advice in making dietary changes and maintaining a good nutritional balance.

MILK AND OTHER DAIRY PRODUCTS

Milk and dairy products play an important part in our diet but can cause an adverse reaction in some people. Depending on the nature of the sensitivity, this may only be a temporary condition and some people may be able to tolerate some dairy products. Luckily, there are many alternative milks and dairy-free products available to ensure that people with a dairy intolerance can enjoy a balanced and varied diet. Always seek medical advice before making any drastic dietary changes because dairy products make a valuable nutritional contribution and shouldn't be excluded without good reason.

WHAT IS LACTOSE INTOLERANCE?

This relatively common condition affects mostly adolescents and adults, and some children. It is more prevalent among Eastern Europeans and people of Asian or African origin, where milk has traditionally played a less important part in the diet after weaning. An intolerance occurs because insufficient lactase enzyme is produced to digest properly the lactose sugar present in milk, so it passes undigested into the large intestine, causing bloating, diarrhea and flatulence.

Lactose intolerance may also occur temporarily following a bout of gastro-enteritis, especially in young children, or as a consequence of gastric surgery or chemotherapy, all of which can destroy lactase production.

Whether you are suffering from a mild or severe, permanent or temporary intolerance, a low-lactose or lactose-free diet is advised, although just how strict it has to be varies between individuals. You may find you can tolerate small amounts of regular milk without ill effect, especially if it is included within a meal, or that you can eat hard cheeses, such as Cheddar, which are low in lactose. Yogurt may be acceptable, too, as the bacteria in yogurt help to digest lactose.

If you or your doctor suspect a lactose intolerance, there are tests that can confirm it. This may involve testing the stools for acidity, which is what usually happens in the case of infants, or measuring blood sugar and breath hydrogen after eating a standard amount of lactose.

ARE YOU ALLERGIC TO MILK?

The number of people who are allergic to cow's milk is unknown but if you suffer from asthma, eczema or rhinitis, dairy products may be the problem.

An elimination and challenge diet procedure is likely to be your best approach for discovering a milk allergy.

FOODS TO AVOID

Dairy products include all types of cow's milk and its derivatives, cream, butter, cheese, quark, yogurt, fromage frais, crème fraîche, evaporated milk, casein (also caseinates and hydrolyzed casein), whey syrup sweetener, hydrolyzed whey protein, whey sugar, non-fat milk solids, lactalbumin and lactose.

If you are following an exclusion diet, you will also need to avoid dishes made using milk. Although you can still enjoy foods such as custard sauces, pancakes, quiches and flans by

Hard cheeses, such as Cheddar, Red Leicester and Parmesan (left), contain less lactose than soft cheeses and may be eaten by some people who are lactose intolerant, as may yogurt (below), which contains bacteria that help to digest lactose.

Above: Many cakes, custard, savory pies and quiches contain dairy products, as do some store-bought sauces.

replacing cow's milk with an alternative "safe" milk. Milk and dairy products are also often hidden ingredients in store-bought foods, such as cakes, cookies, ice cream, chocolate, most margarines and spreads, puddings, dessert mixes, soups and dips.

Some supermarkets may provide lists of milk-free products they carry on request. Look for items labeled "dairy-free" or "suitable for vegans."

KEEPING A HEALTHY NUTRITIONAL BALANCE

Milk and dairy products are usually the main source of calcium in the diet and provide valuable amounts of protein, some B vitamins (particularly B_2/riboflavin) and vitamin A. There are plenty of other foods that can provide calcium and it is important, if you are excluding dairy products either for the short or longer term, that you regularly include a variety of these in your diet. It is vital to maintain an adequate supply of calcium in order to build strong teeth and bones and to help prevent osteoporosis (brittle bone disease) in later life. Check with your doctor or a dietician that your dietary intake is adequate. If it is not, they may recommend that you take a calcium supplement.

Above: Broccoli, leafy greens, sardines, apricots and figs are all good non-dairy sources of calcium.

NON-DAIRY CALCIUM SOURCES
- broccoli and dark green, leafy vegetables
- nuts (especially almonds)
- dried fruits
- seeds
- canned sardines (you need to eat the soft edible bones)
- bread
- dried beans
- soybeans
- tofu
- calcium-fortified soy drinks and cheeses

ALTERNATIVE MILKS

You may need to try several before finding one that suits you, as these too can cause a reaction. Goat's and sheep's milk contain less lactose than cow's milk but are not lactose-free. Other alternative milks include oat drinks, rice drinks and coconut milk.

Goat's milk—This has a slightly tangy taste. Yogurts and a wide range of cheeses are also available.

Sheep's milk—This milk is thicker and creamier than cow's milk because it has a higher fat content. It tastes slightly sweet and is ideal for making pudding.

Soy drinks—Available fresh and in long-life cartons, soy drinks are lactose-free, usually low in fat and can be sweetened, unsweetened and flavored. They are often fortified with calcium and vitamins.

Lactose-reduced milk—This product is made from cow's milk and has had most of the lactose removed.

WATCHPOINT

Alternative milks are not suitable as a main drink for infants under 12 months old. A dietician can advise about specially modified milks that are suitable for the allergic child.

OTHER PROBLEM FOODS

Any food has the potential to cause an allergic reaction or intolerance in susceptible individuals, but certain foods are known to be common allergens.

If you suffer from any of the symptoms associated with food sensitivity, such as rashes, wheezing, abdominal discomfort or migraine, start by investigating the typical suspect foods. If the reaction is immediate, you may be able to identify the culprit fairly easily but if there is a delayed reaction, then this is obviously much more difficult.

Sometimes foods that you particularly like—and therefore eat in large quantities—can be responsible for causing reactions. It could be that you have a sensitivity to the very food you crave.

If you think that a food sensitivity may be the cause of certain symptoms or illness, don't immediately leap to conclusions and start restricting your diet. A detailed investigation is usually necessary before an accurate diagnosis and recommendation can be made, under the supervision of your doctor, dietician or a consultant allergy specialist.

NUTS

Peanuts are a common culprit, as are other nuts, such as walnuts, brazil nuts, hazelnuts and almonds. In cases of extreme allergy, they can trigger "anaphylaxis," which is potentially fatal. Sesame seed allergy, although not as common, can be just as severe. Not all reactions are as violent as anaphylaxis, and milder responses, such as vomiting, urticaria, itchy tongue, coughing and wheezing, can be treated with a fast-acting antihistamine available from a pharmacy.

Nut or sesame allergy is generally a lifelong condition and those with a peanut allergy are likely to have other allergies and suffer from asthma, eczema and/or hay fever.

Nuts are a popular food and are widely used in cakes, cookies, confectionery, marzipan, breakfast cereals, salads and vegetarian foods as well as nut oils (some refined oils are safe) and peanut butter. Many ethnic dishes, such as satay sauce, contain nuts and they're also used in a wide variety of manufactured foods, so you need to check the ingredient labels carefully. Sometimes manufacturers use the warning "may contain nut traces" to cover themselves, but companies are being urged to tighten up production controls and to use accurate labeling.

Foods containing sesame seeds include hummus, tahini, halva, hamburger buns and sesame oil, and they are also widely used in the baking industry.

Above: Many kinds of nuts are associated with food sensitivity but peanuts can cause a severe—sometimes fatal—reaction.

FISH AND SHELLFISH

Healthy eating advice encourages us to enjoy more fish, not only because it is low in saturated fat but because the oily varieties are rich in Omega-3 fatty acids, which are believed to help reduce the risk of heart disease.

However, fish and shellfish can cause an allergic reaction in some people. Fish and shellfish sensitivity are two quite separate problems, so you may find one group of fish are tolerated but not others. Likely symptoms include sickness, diarrhea, abdominal cramps, wheezing, rhinitis, urticaria and dramatic swelling. Simply handling fish, or even just the smell of fish cooking, can trigger symptoms in a sensitive person.

ANAPHYLACTIC SHOCK

This is a the most serious allergic reaction and is life-threatening. It can be caused by fish, sesame seeds, eggs, milk, soy and wheat, wasp or bee stings and some medicines, such as aspirin and penicillin, but the most common is peanut allergy.

Symptoms include facial swelling, shortness of breath, dizziness and loss of consciousness, so it is essential that sufferers are aware of their condition and take every precaution to avoid the offending substance. If you know that you are severely allergic, you should always carry emergency adrenaline treatment. Always inform schools, relatives, friends and anyone who may prepare food for you of your condition. In restaurants, always check with the chef if you are unsure of the ingredients in a dish and, to be on the safe side, order plainly cooked foods. It is also a good idea to wear a pendant or a MedicAlert identification bracelet, stating your food sensitivity, in case there is an emergency. Asthmatics are particularly at risk.

Above: A sensitivity to shellfish is not uncommon and the crustacean group, which includes crabs, lobsters and shrimp, is a frequent culprit.

EGGS

This allergy often co-exists with cow's milk allergy (and sometimes with an allergy to chicken) and is therefore relatively common in young children. However, like cow's milk allergy, the sensitivity frequently disappears by the age of two or three. The protein in the egg white is usually to blame, and allergic symptoms may include urticaria, stomach upsets, wheezing and rhinitis. Egg sensitivity may trigger or worsen eczema and asthma, especially in children.

Foods to be avoided include many cakes, cookies, custard, mayonnaise, hollandaise and Béarnaise sauces, meringues, soufflés, lemon curd, egg noodles, batter mixtures, pancakes, and also some candy and chocolate products. In some recipes the egg or eggs may be simply omitted.

Above: Fresh and dried pasta and noodles, mayonnaise and lemon curd contain eggs.

Check the ingredient labels on manufactured foods for egg white or egg yolk, albumen, egg protein, dried egg and egg lecithin. It is also important to check the labels of meat alternatives.

YEAST

Yeast sensitivity is sometimes blamed for a wide range of complaints, such as fatigue, thrush, stomach bloating, headaches, itchy anus and even PMS (pre-menstrual syndrome). A yeast-free and sugar-free diet is often recommended for this condition, in which case it's necessary to avoid foods containing any form of yeast, mold or fungi, including mushrooms, grapes and mold-ripened cheeses. Bread, pizza, yeasted pastries, yeast extract, beer, wine and cider, dried fruits, vinegar and pickled foods, cheese and fermented dairy products, malted milk drinks, tofu and soy sauce will all be off the menu, and you'll need to check labels for hydrolyzed protein and leavening agents. As yeasts feed on sugar, this needs to be avoided, too.

Soda bread (which uses baking powder or soda as a rising agent), pita, chapatis, matzos, rice cakes and rye crackers provide delicious alternatives to bread. Eating plenty of garlic may help, as it's thought to combat an over-proliferation of yeast in the stomach.

Above: Mushrooms, grapes and mold-ripened cheeses can trigger yeast reactions.

HELP WITH SHOPPING

Most supermarkets and many manufacturers produce "free from" lists for eggs, soy products, peanuts, milk, wheat and gluten.

SOY PRODUCTS

An intolerance to soybean products is relatively common and may occur if there's already a sensitivity to cow's milk. Other members of the bean family, including bean sprouts and peanuts, may also cause a reaction. To follow a totally soy-free diet, check food labels carefully for tofu, lecithin (E322), soy oil, soy sauce, soy beans, textured or hydrolyzed vegetable protein (TVP). Vegetable oil sources should always be checked, as soy oil is often included in blended oils and many vegetarian and gluten-free products may contain soy.

OTHER POSSIBLE CULPRITS

Cheese, chocolate, coffee and citrus fruits (often referred to as the Four Cs) are classic migraine triggers. Alcohol, too, can cause a problem, especially red wine, sherry and port. These foods contain vasoactive amines, which dilate the blood vessels, provoking migraine in susceptible people. Try avoiding these trigger foods and see if the migraines stop, although if you've been a heavy coffee drinker, you may, to begin with, experience headaches caused by caffeine withdrawal. Simple changes to your diet can also help prevent recurrent headaches so be sure to eat regular meals (low blood sugar can precipitate headaches) and drink plenty of water to prevent dehydration.

Strawberries commonly cause urticaria due to the release of histamine soon after eating the fruit. The itchy rash will probably disappear a few hours later.

Citrus fruits (especially oranges) are known to aggravate eczema so avoid these if you have this skin condition.

WHAT ABOUT ADDITIVES?

Additives, especially artificial ones, are often blamed for being the cause of all manner of allergic reactions and may produce behavioral problems, especially in young children, though this is a highly contentious subject. Additives are certainly thought to be responsible for upsetting a minority of susceptible people, but the number affected may well be considerably less than is sometimes suggested.

Additives may be natural (extracted directly from natural products), nature identical (made to match something found in nature) or artificial, but those that are manmade are no more likely to cause adverse reactions than natural additives or, indeed, natural foods. It is important, too, to remember why additives are used in food manufacture. Some are purely cosmetic and are used in response to consumer expectations of color, flavor and texture, but most fulfill important and necessary functions. Without additives, food would not keep as well, so we would have to shop more frequently. There would be a greater risk of food poisoning and we would not be able to enjoy the wide range of convenience foods that we've grown to expect.

WHY ARE ADDITIVES USED?

Additives perform a number of different functions, and they are categorized and grouped according to their function, usually by E number. The E number indicates that the additive has been approved safe by EC regulations. Those listed are the main categories but there are many others, including anti-caking agents, acidity regulators, and so on.

Colors (E100s)—These are used to restore color lost in processing (e.g. canned peas) and to make food look more appetizing. Many are natural colorings, coming from foods such as red bell peppers, grape skins and beets.

Preservatives (E200s)—These help keep food safe for longer by preventing the growth of microorganisms that would cause decay, spoilage and food poisoning. These additives protect our health, reduce waste and allow us to eat a wider choice of foods all year round.

Antioxidants (E300s)—Used to protect fats and oils in food from turning rancid, changing color and deteriorating through oxidation. Vitamin E (E306) is used as a natural antioxidant in vegetable oil and ascorbic acid. In fruit drinks vitamin C (E300) prevents the fruit turning brown.

Emulsifiers and stabilizers (E400s) —Emulsifiers help blend ingredients, such as oil and water, together and stabilizers prevent them from separating again (as in soft margarines and salad dressings). Thickeners and gelling agents add smoothness to the texture.

Flavorings—A complex range of natural flavorings and artificial chemicals are added to various foods. As yet they do not have any serial numbers.

Flavor enhancers—These help bring out the flavor of foods, the most common is MSG (monosodium glutamate/E621). Wherever possible, manufacturers prefer to use stocks, herbs and spices for boosting flavor.

Artificial sweeteners—These are used more and more frequently in place of sugar because they are lower in calories and better for dental health. Saccharin, aspartame and acesulfame-k are the principal artificial intense sweeteners used.

WHICH ADDITIVES MAY BE A PROBLEM?

Preservatives—Some asthmatics are sensitive to sulfites (E220–E227), such as sulfur dioxide. Sulfite preservatives are used in beer, wine and cider but, as yet, alcoholic drinks are exempt from ingredient labeling laws. Sodium benzoate (E211), another preservative used in soft drinks, sweets, jam and margarine, can cause problems for asthma or urticaria sufferers and has been linked with hyperactivity in children.

Artificial colors—These are recognized as upsetting sensitive people, so many manufacturers, acting in response to consumer demand, have reformulated their products to remove them. The azo dyes, which include tartrazine (E102), a yellow color used in soft drinks and crumb coatings, may be particularly troublesome. Tartrazine has been linked with hyperactivity in children and also affects asthmatics. Annatto (E160b), which is a natural color, may also trigger asthma attacks and rashes.

Flavor enhancers—MSG is a widely used flavor enhancer, particularly in Chinese dishes. Some people develop allergic reactions, including headaches, nausea, dizziness and palpitations, on

Above: Alcoholic drinks, such as beer, wine and cider, contain sulfite preservatives but are not subject to ingredient labeling laws.

Above: The flavor enhancer monosodium glutamate (MSG) is often added to Chinese restaurant food.

eating MSG. These reactions have been given the popular name of "Chinese restaurant syndrome." You may want to check with restaurants whether MSG is used and ask for it to be omitted.

HYPERACTIVITY IN CHILDREN
Most children are naturally bounding with energy and can sometimes behave badly. This is all part of growing up and learning social boundaries. It shouldn't be confused with hyperactive behavior, which can be aggressive, unruly and out of control, and makes it virtually impossible for the child to concentrate or settle for long and intolerable for the rest of the family. In some cases, artificial colors and preservatives may be implicated but take advice from a dietician before jumping to conclusions.

AVOIDING ADDITIVES
Most supermarkets produce lists of "additive-free" foods. On packaging stating "no artificial preservatives, colors or flavoring" may also be helpful. Check the labels carefully (all additives must be listed by category and E number or name), and avoid any that you believe cause a reaction. Wherever possible, choose fresh foods.

COULD YOU BE SUFFERING FROM AN ALLERGY?

The first step in finding out whether you have an allergy is to make an appointment with your doctor to discuss your symptoms and rule out other illnesses. True allergies, which usually provoke an immediate and acute reaction, are generally straightforward to diagnose (so the offending food can be avoided), but in most cases of food intolerance, identification can be very much more difficult. (Testing for gluten or lactose intolerance has been discussed under cereals and milk and dairy products.)

DETECTION AND TESTING METHODS USED
There are no quick tests for detecting food intolerances. It is hoped that on-going research projects will provide treatments for allergic conditions and that a greater understanding of the causes will enable better prevention.

The skin prick test and the radio-allergosorbent test (RAST) are the most common tests although even these may give false results.

An elimination and challenge procedure is the best way of discovering which foods are causing a problem, but severe exclusion diets shouldn't be followed long term because they may seriously undermine the nutritional status of the allergy sufferer.

THE SKIN PRICK TEST
In this test, a liquid containing an amount of the suspect allergen is placed on the skin. The skin is then pricked to allow the substance to seep under the surface. If the person undergoing the test is allergic to the substance, histamine is released from the sensitive reactive cells and the skin shows an itchy, red weal.

This test can be useful for identifying environmental allergies, such as pollen or cat hair sensitivity, but is not reliable for food allergy testing or for detecting food intolerances, where the immune system is not involved and where the reaction is often masked or delayed. However, extreme allergic disorders, such as anaphylaxis, do usually give a positive skin prick test.

THE RAST TEST (RADIO-ALLERGOSORBENT TEST)
This test measures IgE antibodies in the blood that allergic people make in reaction to specific substances. It may be helpful for detecting true allergies but not food intolerances.

ELIMINATION DIETS
These diets are the most accurate means of discovering a food intolerance. Suspect foods are eliminated from the person's diet to see if the symptoms subside, then the foods are reintroduced to see if the symptoms return.

Even if you have some idea about which food(s) are causing problems, you should not attempt an exclusion diet on your own, or you may create nutritional deficiencies. Your doctor may refer you to a special hospital unit or a clinic for further investigation or arrange for you to see a dietician if dietary changes are to be considered.

DESENSITIZING METHODS
Some private clinics claim to be able to cure patients of their allergies using a course of injections of a dilute solution of the allergen. As yet, however, these desensitizing methods are not widely recognized by the medical profession.

TESTING FOR FOOD ALLERGIES

Diet investigation is often used to try and discover the cause of food sensitivities. Depending on which food(s) are suspected, the diet may be relatively simple or involve the dieter in a substantial amount of thought and commitment.

In cases of multiple food intolerance, it is far more difficult to discover the whole problem and, because psychological factors may influence a person's perception of how a food affects them, blind testing may be advised so that an accurate diagnosis can be obtained.

Food intolerances are often not lifelong sensitivities. People find that after a rest period the offending food can be reintroduced gradually. However, the food should only be eaten infrequently; eating too much or too often may trigger a repeat of the previous symptoms.

Different clinics and specialists will vary in their approach towards dietary testing, so follow the advice given by your own nutritionist. Whatever the diet, it is essential that you stick to it rigidly as any lapses will affect the validity of your results.

SIMPLE EXCLUSION DIETS

If you have a fairly good idea about which single food is causing you a problem, it is a simple matter to exclude it from your diet and see if the symptoms disappear or improve. It is quite easy to avoid some foods, such as cheese, red wine and citrus fruits, but if a major food group, such as dairy products or wheat is suspected, you will need to take professional advice from a dietician on how to modify your diet safely without missing out on important nutrients. After avoiding the suspect food for a few weeks, try eating it again and see if the symptoms return. If you have experienced a severe allergic reaction to a particular food, such as peanuts, don't attempt to try the food again. You already know the cause of the problem and are strongly advised not to risk repeating the reaction.

Below: Common trigger foods, which cause food intolerances and allergies, include dairy products, such as milk and yogurt, wheat, nuts, citrus fruits and drinks, coffee, chocolate, eggs and shellfish.

ELIMINATION DIET TIPS AND GUIDELINES

● Don't choose a busy time, whether at work or at home, to undertake an elimination diet; you need to be stress-free.
● Prepare and plan ahead, so that you don't run out of suitable foods and can easily provide for other members of the family.
● Do not skip meals.
● Try to base your diet on fresh foods as much as possible.
● Stick to plain cooked dishes because using a lot of ingredients in recipes will make detection all the more difficult.
● Avoid eating out, or if you do, choose plainly cooked dishes.
● Make a note of the ingredients used in any store-bought foods.
● Plan some nonfood treats for yourself, such as a trip to the hairdresser, a manicure or a sauna, so that you don't focus all your attention on your diet.

MULTIPLE FOOD EXCLUSION DIET

If it's suspected that there is a dietary cause for your symptoms but the offending food is not known, it may be suggested that you cut out common trigger foods, which are known to cause problems most frequently. These foods include milk and dairy products, eggs, shellfish, wheat, citrus fruits, nuts, coffee, chocolate and azo dyes and also possibly corn, yeast and soy products.

You will need to follow this diet for two to three weeks to see if any improvement occurs. If symptoms ease or disappear, the excluded foods should

Below: A strict elimination diet permits only foods, such as lamb, turkey, rice, potatoes, broccoli, cauliflower and pears, that rarely cause allergy problems.

then be reintroduced individually, allowing an interval of several days between each. If the symptoms reappear, you have your answer—although several repeat exercises may be necessary to be sure of the diagnosis.

If there is no improvement while following the diet, either some other food could be responsible (and you may be advised to try the more restrictive "few foods" diet) or you will need to investigate other, non-dietary causes.

STRICT ELIMINATION DIET

This very strict diet consists of only a few basic foods that are rarely known to cause a reaction. Because it severely limits the food selection, a strict elimination diet is only advised in extreme cases where medication does not provide any relief. Foods that are commonly allowed include lamb or turkey, potatoes, rice, pears, cauliflower or broccoli (and sometimes other vegetables), sunflower or olive oil and bottled water. The exact range of permitted foods may vary at the discretion of your doctor.

The diet is followed strictly for two to three weeks, then foods are reintroduced one by one, and any change of symptoms observed.

RARE FOODS DIET

This is basically the same as the strict elimination diet, except that some more unusual foods, such as exotic fruits and unusual vegetables and meats, are allowed. The theory behind this diet is that people are less likely to react to foods that they have not eaten (or rarely eaten) before. If symptoms still persist on this diet, then the likely diagnosis is that the person is not food-sensitive and that some other factor is responsible, or that the person has an undiagnosed medical condition.

FASTING

This is a drastic measure that is not generally advised because of the risk of severe nutritional disorders that may

---

FOOD DIARY

Date : *Monday 24th*

Meal	Food / Drink	Time taken	Symptoms
Breakfast	*orange juice* *2 slices of toast* *spread with butter* *& marmalade* *cup of tea*	*7:45am*	
Mid-morning	*cup of coffee* *chocolate cookie*	*10:30am*	
Lunch	*cheese sandwich* *potato chips* *strawberry yogurt*	*12:30pm*	*Migraine about 2:00pm*
Mid-afternoon	*cup of tea* *jelly doughnut*	*3:00pm*	
Evening meal	*grilled fish* *new potatoes and peas* *glass of white wine*	*7:00pm*	

Additional Notes
Difficult day at work—felt very stressed and tired.
Might be starting a cold, sneezing a lot and felt rather stuffed up.

---

affect the balance of your health. It is not advisable to attempt such an extreme regime, whether for intolerance testing, weight loss or any other dietary reason.

KEEPING A FOOD DIARY

Keeping a food diary is useful, both as an initial exercise to find out which foods you eat and whether you are following a healthy, balanced diet, and also when you are following an exclusion or elimination diet.

The food diary can help you discover if you really do have a true food intolerance or sensitivity, or whether your symptoms may have other, non food-related causes. Stress, tiredness and even the menstrual cycle

can all aggravate a condition. Write down everything that you eat and drink, any symptoms that appear, and when or if they worsen.

A detailed food diary will also be a helpful aid for your doctor or dietician when they are trying to reach a diagnosis and may help them see where to make any dietary adjustments. Remember that symptoms may not appear immediately after eating an offending food. Any reaction may happen hours—or even days—later. You can't presume that the culprit is something you ate at your last meal. In addition, a sensitivity reaction to food may be worse one day than another. All this makes the detection process quite difficult, so you will need to be both vigilant and patient.

ALLERGY-FREE EATING

If you have a food sensitivity and need to follow a restricted diet, it does not mean that your food has to be boring. With the fantastic choice of multi-cultural foods, exotic fresh fruits and vegetables and an increasing range of organic produce available from supermarkets and health food shops, there will always be plenty of foods to replace those that you may need to avoid.

EATING OUT

A food sensitivity does not mean that you can't eat out anymore, but you will have to think ahead, do a little planning and inform anyone who will be cooking for you and needs to know about any problem foods.

Exactly how careful you need to be will depend on the nature of your sensitivity and the severity of the reaction. Some foods, such as fish, oranges, tomatoes or strawberries, are easy to avoid, while others, such as wheat or dairy products, will be more difficult because they are common ingredients used in a wide variety of dishes. If you suffer from a severe allergy, such as peanut anaphylaxis, it is absolutely essential that you avoid the offending food.

DINING INVITATIONS

If you have been invited to a friend's home for a meal, it is polite and considerate to warn your host if there's something you are unable to eat. If you are vegetarian, for example, you would inform your host beforehand to avoid any embarrassment, and the same applies to food intolerances.

If you feel that this creates any difficulty for your host, then offer to contribute a dish, such as a dessert, towards the meal to make the cooking easier. If you should be served something that you know will disagree with you, don't worry about refusing it, simply explain tactfully exactly why you are unable to eat the offending food.

RESTAURANT MEALS

Be selective about where you eat and choose restaurants that prepare fresh food. In restaurants where the dishes are brought in already-prepared, the

Above: When you are dining out, choose simply cooked foods so that you can see exactly what you are eating.

chef or kitchen staff may not have detailed knowledge of the ingredients used in the food.

It may sometimes be advisable to ask to see the menu in advance, then discuss any special dietary requests with the chef. Don't wait until the restaurant is busy or expect a waiter

Below: Eggs are widely used for thickening and enriching sauces and desserts, binding ground meats and glazing pastries.

to have an in-depth knowledge of how dishes have been prepared.

Campaigns about the dangers of severe food allergies have alerted chefs to be aware of the ingredients they use—particularly nuts, seeds and shellfish—and to be helpful should a customer ask about the ingredients in a dish. If there are any doubts or the chef isn't available, don't guess and trust to luck or try to pick out offending ingredients. Choose a dish that you can rely on to be safe.

WHAT TO CHOOSE

Composite dishes and sauces that contain lots of ingredients are probably best avoided. If you're in a hurry, and haven't time to ask questions, the best option is to choose something simple: plain cooked foods, such as grilled, baked or roasted fish, meat or poultry accompanied by fresh vegetables or a salad, followed by fresh fruit.

SOME DISHES TO AVOID

● Foods that may contain either nuts or seeds, such as marzipan, cakes, breads, cookies and cheesecakes, hummus, pesto sauce, salad dressings, satay sauce and many vegetarian dishes.
● Indian and Chinese dishes, such as tandoori and tikka dishes, rice pilaf, spare ribs, and sweet-and-sour pork, which may contain artificial colors.
● Asian foods, which may contain sesame oil.
● Stews, sauces and soups, which may be thickened with wheat flour.
● Foods, such as sausages, fish sticks and chicken nuggets, which may contain bread crumbs.
● Foods that contain "hidden" eggs used for binding, thickening, coating, setting, enriching or glazing.

COOKING FOR CHILDREN

Children are notorious for being picky about food, but it's important not to confuse fussy eating with food allergies and intolerances, which actually trigger a very real physical reaction. Inheritance seems to be a factor in predisposing a child to suffering from allergies. This tendency, in which a family may suffer from various allergies, is known as atopy. Although children often outgrow childhood allergies, such as asthma and eczema, those with a family history of allergic illness are more likely to develop other allergic conditions and possibly food intolerance problems.

COMMON ALLERGIES

Milk allergy can start in early infancy when a formula milk or cow's milk is introduced during weaning. The most common symptoms are asthma, eczema, urticaria, allergic rhinitis, vomiting and diarrhea. Breastfeeding may help to prevent the condition, especially where there is a family history of allergic illness. Lactose intolerance may also occur temporarily following a bout of gastroenteritis in young children. On recovery from illness, and after excluding lactose for a while, the condition usually clears up but always take advice from your doctor. Most children outgrow any sensitivity to cow's milk by the age of three years.

Wheat and eggs are also common foods to which children may have a sensitivity, generally showing as asthma or eczema. To reduce the risk of allergies, these foods should not be introduced too early into an infant's diet. It is recommended that wheat and egg yolk are not introduced before six months, egg white not until nine months, and regular cow's milk ideally not before one year. Rice is considered to be the least "allergenic" cereal and is recommended as a weaning food from the age of four months. Look out for the gluten-free symbol on store-bought baby foods and don't be tempted to introduce solids into your baby's diet too early.

If a child does develop an allergy while weaning, always seek professional advice and never attempt an elimination diet without expert guidance. Most children outgrow such problems by the age of five.

HEALTHY EATING

A child's diet should be well balanced nutritionally, and meet all his or her requirements for energy, growth, repair and maintenance. The foods don't have to be exclusively healthy—"junk" foods can be very appealing to a child and need not be banned, provided they are not eaten in place of healthier fresh food alternatives and are not the cause of any allergic condition.

If your child does have any food sensitivities, try not to make a fuss about any special diets. Make meals fun and enjoyable, and help your child develop a healthy interest in food by encouraging him or her to help with the shopping and meal preparation.

SCHOOL LUNCHES

If you prepare bag lunches for your child, and some foods are not allowed, make sure your child understands why

Above: Young children can often be persuaded to try adult food if the family sits down together and makes the mealtime into a social occasion.

he or she should not swap items with friends. If the child is to eat a cooked school meal at lunchtime, talk to the school food service, who are generally happy to discuss and provide for special needs. Although most school food services no longer use nuts or seeds, you should always inform the school of any severe allergies.

ARE ADDITIVES TO BLAME?

If you think that additives (particularly colorings and preservatives) are causing an allergic reaction or making your child behave badly, then the best policy is to feed the child simple, fresh foods and to cook your own homemade dishes.

SOUPS, APPETIZERS AND SALADS

*Whatever the season or the occasion, you will find a recipe here to
enhance your meal. There's a range of delicious nutritious snacks,
light lunches and elegant appetizers to tempt you. Lentil Soup with
Tomatoes or Spicy Potato Wedges with Chili Dip will warm you on a
winter day. Chilled Summer Tomato Soup or Prosciutto with Mango
will bring Mediterranean flavors to your table in midsummer.*

Lentil Soup with Tomatoes

A classic rustic Italian soup flavored with rosemary.

INGREDIENTS

Serves 4

1 cup dried green or
　brown lentils
3 tablespoons extra-virgin olive oil
3 lean slices bacon, diced into
　small pieces
1 onion, finely chopped
2 celery stalks, finely chopped
2 carrots, finely diced
2 rosemary sprigs, finely chopped
2 bay leaves
14-ounce can chopped plum tomatoes
7½ cups vegetable stock
salt and ground black pepper
bay leaves and rosemary sprigs,
　to garnish

1 Place the lentils in a bowl and cover with cold water. Let soak for 2 hours. Rinse and drain well.

2 Heat the oil in a large saucepan. Add the bacon and cook for about 3 minutes, then stir in the onion and cook for 5 minutes, until softened. Stir in the celery, carrots, rosemary, bay leaves and lentils. Toss over the heat for 1 minute, until thoroughly coated in the oil.

3 Add the tomatoes and stock and bring to a boil. Lower the heat, half cover the pan, and simmer for about 1 hour or until the lentils are perfectly tender.

4 Remove the bay leaves, add salt and pepper to taste and serve with a garnish of fresh bay leaves and rosemary sprigs.

NUTRITION NOTES	
Per portion:	
Calories	357
Protein	19.6g
Fat	16.6g
Saturated fat	3.9g
Carbohydrate	34.7g
Sugar	6.63g
Fiber (NSP)	6.8g
Calcium	80mg

Spinach and Rice Soup

Use very fresh, young spinach leaves to prepare this light and clean-tasting soup.

INGREDIENTS

Serves 4

1½ pounds fresh spinach, washed
3 tablespoons extra-virgin olive oil
1 small onion, finely chopped
2 garlic cloves, finely chopped
1 small fresh red chile, seeded and
　finely chopped
generous 1 cup arborio rice
5 cups vegetable stock
salt and ground black pepper
¼ cup freshly grated Parmesan cheese,
　to serve

1 Place the spinach in a large pan with just the water that clings to its leaves after washing. Add a large pinch of salt. Heat gently until the spinach has wilted, then remove from heat and drain, reserving any liquid.

2 Either chop the spinach finely using a large knife or place in a food processor and process to a fairly coarse purée.

3 Heat the oil in a large saucepan and cook the onion, garlic and chile for 4–5 minutes, until softened. Stir in the rice, then pour in the stock and the reserved spinach liquid. Bring to a boil, then simmer for 10 minutes. Add the spinach and season to taste. Cook for 5–7 more minutes, until the rice is tender. Serve with Parmesan cheese.

NUTRITION NOTES	
Per portion:	
Calories	292
Protein	12.6g
Fat	14.8g
Saturated fat	4.4g
Carbohydrate	29.5g
Sugar	3.16g
Fiber (NSP)	3.8g
Calcium	470mg

Summer Tomato Soup

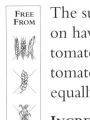

FREE FROM

The success of this soup depends on having ripe, full-flavored tomatoes, so make it when the tomato season is at its peak. It is equally delicious served cold.

INGREDIENTS

Serves 4
1 tablespoon olive oil
1 large onion, chopped
1 carrot, chopped
2¼ pounds ripe tomatoes, cored and quartered
2 garlic cloves, chopped
5 thyme sprigs, or ¼ teaspoon dried thyme
4 or 5 marjoram sprigs, or ¼ teaspoon dried marjoram
1 bay leaf
3 tablespoons sheep's or goat's milk yogurt, plus a little extra to garnish
salt and ground black pepper
marjoram sprigs, to garnish

1 Heat the olive oil in a large, nonreactive, saucepan or flameproof casserole.

2 Add the onion and carrot and cook for 3–4 minutes, until just softened, stirring occasionally.

VARIATION

To serve the soup cold, omit the yogurt and let cool, then chill.

---

3 Add the tomatoes, garlic and herbs. Reduce the heat and simmer, covered, for 30 minutes.

4 Pass the soup through a food mill or press through a sieve into the pan. Stir in the yogurt and season. Reheat gently and serve in warmed soup bowls, garnished with a spoonful of yogurt and a sprig of marjoram.

NUTRITION NOTES	
Per portion:	
Calories	84
Protein	2.4g
Fat	4g
Saturated fat	0.9g
Carbohydrate	10.2g
Sugar	9.8g
Fiber (NSP)	3g
Calcium	39mg

Pumpkin Soup

FREE FROM

INGREDIENTS

Serves 6–8
2 tablespoons margarine
1 large onion, chopped
2 shallots, chopped
2 medium potatoes, peeled and cubed
6 cups cubed pumpkin
8 cups chicken or vegetable stock
½ teaspoon ground cumin
pinch of freshly grated nutmeg
salt and ground black pepper
fresh parsley or chives, to garnish

1 Melt the margarine in a large flameproof casserole or saucepan. Add the onion and shallots and cook for 4–5 minutes, until just softened.

2 Add the potatoes, pumpkin, stock, cumin and grated nutmeg, and season with a little salt and black pepper. Reduce the heat to low and simmer, covered, for about 1 hour, stirring occasionally, until the vegetables are thoroughly cooked.

NUTRITION NOTES	
Per portion:	
Calories	71–95
Protein	2.4–3.2g
Fat	3.5–4.6g
Saturated fat	1.5–1.9g
Carbohydrate	8.7–10.9g
Sugar	2.9–3.9g
Fiber (NSP)	1.6–2.1g
Calcium	41–55mg

3 With a slotted spoon, transfer the cooked vegetables to a food processor and process until smooth, adding a little of the cooking liquid if needed. Stir the purée into the cooking liquid remaining in the pan until well mixed. Adjust the seasoning and reheat gently. Garnish the soup with the fresh herbs.

Melon and Grapefruit Cocktail

FREE FROM

This pretty, colorful appetizer can be made in minutes, so it is perfect for when you don't have much time to cook but want something really special to eat.

INGREDIENTS

Serves 4

1 small Galia or
   Ogen melon
1 small Charentais melon
2 pink grapefruit
3 tablespoons freshly squeezed
   orange juice
¼ cup red vermouth
seeds from ½ pomegranate
mint sprigs, to decorate

— COOK'S TIP —

If citrus fruits are a problem, substitute other fruits, such as kiwi fruits, and use apple juice in place of the orange.

1 Halve the melons and scoop out the seeds. Cut into wedges, peel, then cut into large bite-size pieces.

— NUTRITION NOTES —

Per portion:

Calories	52
Protein	0.8g
Fat	0.2g
Saturated fat	0g
Carbohydrate	9.4g
Sugar	9.4g
Fiber (NSP)	1.1g
Calcium	24mg

2 Using a small sharp knife, cut the peel and pith from the grapefruit. Holding the fruit over a bowl to catch the juice, cut between the grapefruit membranes to release the segments. Pour off all the juice into a bowl.

3 Stir the orange juice and vermouth into the reserved grapefruit juice.

4 Arrange the melon pieces and grapefruit segments haphazardly on four individual serving plates. Spoon the dressing over, then scatter with the pomegranate seeds. Decorate with mint sprigs and serve immediately.

Prosciutto with Mango

FREE FROM

Other fresh, colorful fruits, such as figs, papayas or melons, would go equally well with the prosciutto in this light, elegant appetizer. Be sure to buy the true prosciutto from Parma for the best flavor. This dish is amazingly simple to prepare and can be made in advance—ideal if you are serving a complicated main course.

INGREDIENTS

Serves 4

16 slices prosciutto
1 ripe mango
ground black pepper
flat-leaf parsley sprigs, to garnish

1 Separate the prosciutto slices and arrange four slices on each of four individual plates, crumpling the ham slightly to give a decorative effect.

2 Cut the mango into three thick slices around the pit, then slice the flesh and discard the pit. Neatly cut away the skin from each slice.

3 Arrange the mango slices in among the prosciutto slices. Grind some black pepper over the top and serve garnished with flat-leaf parsley sprigs.

— NUTRITION NOTES —

Per portion:

Calories	73
Protein	6.6g
Fat	2.75g
Saturated fat	1.4g
Carbohydrate	4.7g
Sugar	4.6g
Fiber (NSP)	0.8g
Calcium	7mg

Spicy Potato Wedges with Chili Dip

Perfect as an appetizer or light meal, these dry-roasted potato wedges have a crisp, spicy crust, which makes them irresistible, especially when served with a chili dip.

INGREDIENTS

Serves 2
2 baking potatoes, about
    8 ounces each
2 tablespoons olive oil
2 garlic cloves, crushed
1 teaspoon ground allspice
1 teaspoon ground coriander
1 tablespoon paprika
sea salt and ground black pepper

For the dip
1 tablespoon olive oil
1 small onion, finely chopped
1 garlic clove, crushed
7-ounce can chopped tomatoes
1 fresh red chile, seeded and
    finely chopped
1 tablespoon lemon juice
1 tablespoon chopped fresh cilantro,
    plus extra to garnish

1 Preheat the oven to 400°F. Cut the potatoes in half, then into eight wedges.

2 Place the wedges in a saucepan of cold water. Bring to a boil, then lower the heat and simmer gently for 10 minutes or until softened slightly. Drain and pat dry on paper towels.

COOK'S TIP

To save time, parboil the potatoes and toss them with the spices in advance, but make sure that the potato wedges are perfectly dry and completely covered in the mixture.

3 Combine the oil, garlic, allspice, coriander and paprika in a roasting pan. Add salt and pepper to taste. Add the potatoes to the pan and shake to coat them thoroughly.

4 Roast the potato wedges for about 20 minutes, turning them occasionally, until they are browned, crisp and fully cooked.

5 Meanwhile, make the chili dip. Heat the oil in a saucepan, add the onion and garlic and cook for 5–10 minutes, until soft. Add the canned tomatoes, with their juice, then stir in the chile and lemon juice.

6 Cook gently for 10 minutes, until the mixture has reduced and thickened. Stir in the fresh cilantro and serve hot, with the potato wedges. Garnish the potato wedges with fresh cilantro and sprinkle with salt.

--- NUTRITION NOTES ---

Per portion:
Calories	344
Protein	6.1g
Fat	17g
Saturated fat	2.3g
Carbohydrate	44.1g
Sugar	5.8g
Fiber (NSP)	40g
Calcium	31mg

Globe Artichokes, Green Beans and Garlic Dressing

Similar to French aïoli, but egg-free and exceptionally garlicky, this creamy, lemon-flavored dressing makes a perfect partner to freshly cooked vegetables.

INGREDIENTS

Serves 4–6
8 ounces green beans
3 small globe artichokes
1 tablespoon olive oil
pared zest of 1 lemon
coarse salt for sprinkling
lemon wedges, to serve

For the garlic dressing
6 large garlic cloves, sliced
2 teaspoons lemon juice
1 cup extra-virgin olive oil
salt and ground black pepper

1 To make the garlic dressing, put the garlic and lemon juice in a blender or mini food processor. With the machine switched on, gradually pour in the olive oil until the mixture is thickened and smooth. Alternatively, crush the garlic to a paste with the lemon juice and gradually beat in the oil using a hand whisk. Season with salt and pepper to taste.

2 To make the salad, cook the beans in boiling water for 1–2 minutes, until slightly softened. Drain.

3 Trim the artichoke stalks close to the bottom. Cook the artichokes in a large pan of salted water for about 30 minutes or until you can easily pull off a leaf from the bottom. Drain well.

--- COOK'S TIP ---

Mediterranean baby artichokes are sometimes available and are perfect for this kind of salad because, unlike the larger ones, they can be eaten whole. Cook them until just tender, then cut in half to serve. Canned artichoke hearts, thoroughly drained and sliced, can also be used.

4 Using a sharp knife, halve the artichokes lengthwise and remove the choke using a teaspoon.

5 Arrange the artichokes and beans on serving plates and drizzle with the oil. Scatter with the lemon zest and season with coarse salt and a little pepper. Spoon the dressing into the artichoke hearts and serve warm with lemon wedges. To eat artichokes, pull the leaves from the base one at a time and use to scoop a little of the sauce. It is only the fleshy end of each leaf that is eaten as well as the base or "heart" of the artichoke.

--- NUTRITION NOTES ---

Per portion:

Calories	282–416
Protein	2.2–3.4g
Fat	29.6–44.4g
Saturated fat	4.2g–6.4g
Carbohydrate	2.7–4.1g
Sugar	1.6–2.4g
Fiber (NSP)	0.8–1.2g
Calcium	36–54mg

Olives with Spicy Marinades

INGREDIENTS

Serves 6–8

1⅓ cups green or tan olives for
    each marinade

For the spicy herb marinade
3 tablespoons chopped fresh cilantro
3 tablespoons chopped fresh flat-
    leaf parsley
1 garlic clove, finely chopped
good pinch of cayenne pepper
good pinch of ground cumin
2–3 tablespoons extra-virgin olive oil
2–3 tablespoons lemon juice

For the ginger and chili marinade
¼ cup chopped fresh cilantro
¼ cup chopped fresh flat-
    leaf parsley
1 garlic clove, finely chopped
1 teaspoon grated fresh ginger
1 red chile, seeded and finely sliced
¼ preserved lemon, cut into thin
    strips (optional)

1 Squash the olives, hard enough to break the flesh, but taking care not to crack the pit. Place in a bowl of cold water and let sit overnight to remove the excess brine.

2 Drain thoroughly and divide the olives between two jars.

3 Blend the ingredients for the spicy herb marinade and pour into one of the jars of olives, adding more oil and lemon juice to cover, if necessary. Seal the jar.

4 To make the ginger and chili marinade, combine the cilantro, parsley, garlic, ginger, chile and preserved lemon, if using. Add to the remaining jar of olives and seal.

5 Store the olives in the refrigerator for at least one week before use, shaking the jars occasionally.

— NUTRITION NOTES —

Per portion:

Calories	66–88
Protein	0.3–0.4g
Fat	7.2–9.6g
Saturated fat	1.1–1.4g
Carbohydrate	0.1–0.12g
Sugar	0.1–0.12g
Fiber (NSP)	0.35–0.5g
Calcium	17–23mg

Fava Bean Dip

This dish is similar to hummus, but uses fava beans instead of chickpeas. It is usually eaten by scooping up the purée with bread, but raw vegetable crudités or potato chips could be served for dipping.

INGREDIENTS

Serves 6–8

4 ounces dried fava beans, soaked
2 garlic cloves, peeled
1 teaspoon cumin seed
about ¼ cup olive oil
salt
mint sprigs, to garnish
extra cumin seeds, cayenne pepper and
    vegetables crudités to serve

1 Put the dried fava beans in a pan with the whole garlic cloves and cumin seed and add enough water just to cover. Bring to a boil, then reduce the heat and simmer until the beans are tender. Drain, cool and then slip off the outer skin of each bean.

2 Purée the beans in a food processor or blender, adding sufficient olive oil and water to give a smooth soft dip. Season to taste with plenty of salt. Garnish with sprigs of mint and serve with extra cumin seed, cayenne pepper and vegetables crudités.

— NUTRITION NOTES —

Per portion:

Calories	114–171
Protein	5–7.5g
Fat	7.9–11.8g
Saturated fat	1.1–1.7g
Carbohydrate	6.2–9.3g
Sugar	1.1–1.6g
Fiber (NSP)	5.3–7.9g
Calcium	19.1–28.7mg

Spanish Rice Salad

This rice salad is packed with the flavors of the Mediterranean and would make a good accompaniment to all sorts of fish, poultry and meat dishes.

INGREDIENTS

Serves 4

10 ounces long-grain rice
1 bunch scallions, finely sliced
1 green bell pepper, seeded and diced
1 yellow bell pepper, seeded and diced
½ pound tomatoes, peeled, seeded and chopped
2 tablespoons fresh chopped cilantro

For the dressing

5 tablespoons mixed sunflower and olive oil
1 tablespoon rice vinegar
1 teaspoon Dijon mustard
salt and ground black pepper

1 Cook the rice for 10–12 minutes, until tender but still slightly firm. Do not overcook. Drain and rinse with cold water.

— COOK'S TIP —

Cooked peas, cooked diced carrot and/or canned or frozen corn could be added to this adaptable salad.

2 Let the rice cool completely and then place in a large serving bowl. Add the scallions, peppers, tomatoes and cilantro.

3 Make the dressing by putting all the ingredients in a jar with a tight-fitting lid and shaking vigorously until well blended. Stir the dressing into the rice and adjust the seasoning.

4 Cover and chill for about 1 hour before serving.

— NUTRITION NOTES —

Per portion:	
Calories	275
Protein	4.3g
Fat	11.1g
Saturated fat	1.8g
Carbohydrate	42g
Sugar	2.8g
Fiber (NSP)	1.6g
Calcium	37mg

Salad Niçoise

There are probably as many versions of this salad as there are cooks in Provence. This regional classic makes a wonderful lunch or appetizer for a big meal.

INGREDIENTS

Serves 4

8 ounces green beans, trimmed
1 pound new potatoes, peeled and cut
  into 1-inch pieces
white wine vinegar and olive oil,
  for sprinkling
1 small Romaine or Boston lettuce
4 ripe plum tomatoes, quartered
1 small cucumber, peeled, seeded
  and sliced
1 green or red bell pepper, thinly sliced
4 eggs, hard-boiled, peeled
  and quartered
24 black olives
8-ounce can tuna in water, drained
2-ounce can anchovies, drained
basil leaves, to garnish

For the dressing

1 tablespoon Dijon mustard
2-ounce can anchovies, drained
1 garlic clove, crushed
¼ cup lemon juice
½ cup sunflower oil
½ cup extra virgin
  olive oil
salt and ground black pepper

NUTRITION NOTES	
Per portion:	
Calories	319
Protein	18.2g
Fat	25.3g
Saturated fat	3.4g
Carbohydrate	4.6g
Sugar	4.3g
Fiber (NSP)	2.3g
Calcium	81mg

1 To make the dressing, place the mustard, anchovies and garlic in a bowl and blend together by pressing the garlic and anchovies against the sides of the bowl. Season generously with pepper. Using a small whisk, blend in the lemon juice or wine vinegar. Slowly whisk in the sunflower oil in a thin stream and then the olive oil, whisking until the dressing is smooth and creamy.

2 Tip the green beans into a saucepan of salted boiling water and cook for 3 minutes, until tender, yet crisp. Transfer to a colander with a slotted spoon then rinse under cold running water. Drain again and set aside.

3 Add the potatoes to the same boiling water, reduce the heat and simmer for 10-15 minutes, until just tender, then drain. Sprinkle with a little vinegar and olive oil and a spoonful of the dressing.

4 Arrange the lettuce on a platter, top with the tomatoes, cucumber and pepper, then add the cooked beans and potatoes.

5 Arrange the eggs, olives, tuna and anchovies on top, distributing them evenly, and garnish with the basil leaves. Drizzle the remaining dressing over the top.

FREE FROM

Greek Salad

Use a soy-based alternative to feta cheese if you prefer.

INGREDIENTS

Serves 6

1 small Romaine lettuce, sliced
1 pound tomatoes, cut into eighths
1 cucumber, seeded and chopped
7 ounces feta cheese, crumbled
4 scallions, sliced
½ cup black olives, pitted
   and halved

For the dressing

6 tablespoons extra virgin olive oil
1½ tablespoons lemon juice
salt and ground black pepper

1 Put the lettuce, tomatoes, cucumber, feta cheese, scallions and olives into a large bowl.

2 To make the dressing, whisk together the olive oil and lemon juice, then season with salt and pepper.

3 Pour the dressing over the salad. Toss gently until the ingredients are lightly coated in the dressing, then serve immediately.

NUTRITION NOTES	
Per portion:	
Calories	215
Protein	6.6g
Fat	19.1g
Saturated fat	6.4g
Carbohydrate	4.3g
Sugar	4.2g
Fiber (NSP)	1.8g
Calcium	148mg

Spiced Eggplant Salad

This Middle-Eastern style salad can be served with warm pita bread as an appetizer or light lunch dish or to accompany a main course rice pilaf. Choose the type of yogurt that will suit your diet, or omit it altogether.

INGREDIENTS

Serves 4

2 small eggplant, sliced
5 tablespoons olive oil
¼ cup red wine vinegar
2 garlic cloves, crushed
1 tablespoon lemon juice
½ teaspoon ground cumin
½ teaspoon ground coriander
½ cucumber, thinly sliced
2 tomatoes, thinly sliced
2 tablespoons plain yogurt, to serve
   (optional)
salt and ground black pepper
chopped flat-leaf parsley, to garnish

1 Preheat the broiler. Brush the eggplant slices lightly with some of the oil and cook under high heat, turning once, until golden and tender.

2 Cut the cooked eggplant slices into quarters.

3 Combine the remaining oil, vinegar, garlic, lemon juice, cumin and coriander. Season with salt and pepper and mix thoroughly. Add the warm eggplant, stir well and chill for at least 2 hours.

4 Add the cucumber and tomatoes and mix well. Transfer to a serving dish and spoon the yogurt on top, if using.

NUTRITION NOTES	
Per portion:	
Calories	148
Protein	1.5g
Fat	14.2g
Saturated fat	2.11g
Carbohydrate	3.8g
Sugar	3.6g
Fiber (NSP)	1.92g
Calcium	29.7mg

Black and Orange Salad

The darkness of the olives contrasts with the brightness of the orange wedges in this attractive salad.

INGREDIENTS

Serves 4

3 oranges
1 cup black olives, pitted
1 tablespoon chopped fresh cilantro
1 tablespoon chopped fresh parsley
2 tablespoons olive oil
1 tablespoon lemon juice
½ teaspoon paprika
½ teaspoon ground cumin

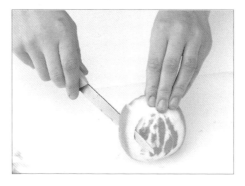

1 Cut away the peel and pith from the oranges and cut into wedges.

2 Place the oranges in a salad bowl and add the black olives, cilantro and parsley.

3 Blend together the olive oil, lemon juice, paprika and cumin. Pour the dressing over the salad and toss gently. Chill for about 30 minutes and serve.

NUTRITION NOTES	
Per portion:	
Calories	120
Protein	1.5g
Fat	8.8g
Saturated fat	1.3g
Carbohydrate	9.2g
Sugar	9.2g
Fiber (NSP)	2.7g
Calcium	69mg

Arugula and Cilantro Salad

Arugula has a wonderful, peppery flavor and, mixed with cilantro, makes a delicious green salad. However, unless you grow your own arugula, or have access to a plentiful supply, you may well have to use extra spinach or another green leaf in order to pad this salad out.

INGREDIENTS

Serves 4

4 ounces or more arugula leaves
4 ounces young spinach leaves
1 large bunch (about 1 ounce)
    fresh cilantro, chopped
2–3 fresh parsley sprigs, chopped
1 garlic clove, crushed
3 tablespoons olive oil
2 teaspoons white wine vinegar
pinch of paprika
cayenne pepper
salt

1 Place the arugula and spinach leaves in a salad bowl. Add the chopped cilantro and parsley.

2 In a small cup, blend together the garlic, olive oil, vinegar, paprika, cayenne pepper and salt.

3 Pour the dressing over the salad, toss lightly, then serve immediately.

NUTRITION NOTES	
Per portion:	
Calories	88
Protein	1.6g
Fat	8.7g
Saturated fat	1.2g
Carbohydrate	0.9g
Sugar	0.8g
Fiber (NSP)	1.2g
Calcium	97mg

Meat and Poultry

Whether your preference is for lamb, beef, pork or chicken, you're bound to find a recipe here to please. From exotic Middle Eastern Lamb Tagine, subtly flavored with spices, through deliciously rich Beef Rolls with Garlic and Tomato Sauce, to simple but succulent Spiced Grilled Poussins, there are dishes to suit every taste and time of year. Pork Tenderloin with Sage and Orange makes a speedy mid-week supper, while Spiced Duck with Pears is the perfect choice for guests.

Lamb Tagine

INGREDIENTS

Serves 4
½ cup dried apricots
2 tablespoons olive oil
1 large onion, chopped
2¼ pounds boneless shoulder of
   lamb, cubed
1 teaspoon ground cumin
1 teaspoon ground coriander
1 teaspoon ground cinnamon
grated zest and juice of ½ orange
1 teaspoon saffron strands
1 tablespoon ground almonds
1¼ cups lamb or chicken stock
1 tablespoon sesame seeds
salt and ground black pepper
fresh parsley, to garnish
couscous, to serve

1 Cut the apricots in half and put in a bowl with ⅔ cup water. Let soak overnight.

2 Preheat the oven to 350°F. Heat the olive oil in a flameproof casserole. Add the onion and cook gently for 10 minutes, until soft and golden.

3 Stir in the lamb. Add the cumin, coriander and cinnamon, with salt and pepper to taste. Stir to coat the lamb cubes in the spices, then cook, stirring, for 5 minutes.

4 Add the apricots and their soaking liquid. Stir in the orange zest and juice, saffron, ground almonds and enough stock to cover. Cover the casserole and cook for 1–1½ hours, until the meat is tender, stirring occasionally and adding extra stock if necessary.

5 Meanwhile, heat a heavy frying pan, add the sesame seeds and dry-fry, shaking the pan, until the seeds are golden. Sprinkle the sesame seeds over the meat, garnish with parsley and serve with couscous.

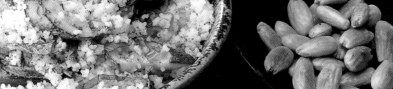

— COOK'S TIP —

Substitute rice for the couscous and this dish will be both wheat- and gluten-free.

— NUTRITION NOTES —

Per portion:
Calories	598
Protein	56g
Fat	35g
Saturated fat	12.1g
Carbohydrate	14.2g
Sugar	13.6g
Fiber (NSP)	3.4g
Calcium	111mg

Lamb Pie with Mustard-Potato Crust

INGREDIENTS

Serves 4

1¾ pounds russet potatoes, diced
1 tablespoon whole-grain mustard
a little margarine
1 pound ground lean lamb
1 onion, chopped
2 celery stalks, thinly sliced
2 carrots, diced
2 tablespoons cornstarch
⅔ cup beef stock
1 tablespoon vegetarian Worcestershire
   sauce
2 tablespoons chopped fresh rosemary,
   or 2 teaspoons dried
salt and ground black pepper
fresh vegetables, to serve

1 Cook the potatoes in boiling lightly salted water until tender. Drain well and mash until smooth, then stir in the mustard, margarine and seasoning to taste. Meanwhile, preheat the oven to 400°F.

2 Brown the lamb in a nonstick pan, breaking it up with a fork. Add the onion, celery and carrots to the pan and cook for 2–3 minutes, stirring.

3 Blend together the cornstarch and stock and stir into the lamb mixture. Bring to a boil, stirring, then remove from heat. Add the Worcestershire sauce and rosemary and season with salt and pepper.

4 Transfer the lamb mixture to a 7½ cup ovenproof dish and spread the potato topping over evenly, swirling with the edge of a knife. Bake for 30–35 minutes, until golden. Serve hot with fresh vegetables.

NUTRITION NOTES

Per portion:

Calories	371
Protein	28g
Fat	13.7g
Saturated fat	6.8g
Carbohydrate	36g
Sugar	4.5g
Fiber (NSP)	3.5g
Calcium	177mg

--- COOK'S TIP ---

Vegetarian Worcestershire sauce, which doesn't contain anchovies, is available at health food stores.

FREE FROM

Green Peppercorn- and Cinnamon-Crusted Lamb

FREE FROM

Racks of lamb are perfect for dinner parties. This version has a spiced crumb coating.

INGREDIENTS

Serves 6

2 ounces ciabatta bread
1 tablespoon drained green peppercorns in brine, lightly crushed
1 tablespoon ground cinnamon
1 garlic clove, crushed
½ teaspoon salt
2 tablespoons margarine, melted
2 teaspoons Dijon mustard
2 racks of lamb, trimmed
1⅔ cups lamb stock
2 tablespoons tomato paste
fresh vegetables, to serve

1 Preheat the oven to 425°F. Break the ciabatta bread into pieces, spread out on a baking sheet and bake for about 10 minutes or until pale golden. Let cool, then process the bread in a blender or food processor to make fine crumbs.

2 Place the crumbs in a bowl and add the green peppercorns, cinnamon, garlic and salt. Stir in the melted margarine. Spread the mustard over the lamb. Press the crumb mixture into the mustard to make a thin, even crust. Put the racks in a roasting pan and roast for 30 minutes, covering the ends with foil if they start to brown too quickly.

3 Remove the lamb to a carving board, cover with loosely tented foil and keep hot.

4 Skim the fat from the juices in the roasting pan. Stir in the stock and tomato paste. Bring to a boil, stirring in any sediment, then lower the heat and simmer until reduced to a rich gravy. Carve the lamb and serve with the gravy and vegetables.

NUTRITION NOTES	
Per portion:	
Calories	414
Protein	53.1g
Fat	27.0g
Saturated fat	11.3g
Carbohydrate	3.1g
Sugar	1.1g
Fiber (NSP)	1.5g
Calcium	26mg

Lamb Casserole with Garlic and Fava Beans

This Spanish-influenced recipe makes a substantial meal, served with mashed potatoes.

INGREDIENTS

Serves 6

3 tablespoons olive oil
3–3½ pounds lamb fillet, cut into
   2-inch cubes
1 large onion, chopped
6 large garlic cloves, unpeeled
1 bay leaf
1 teaspoon paprika
½ cup lamb stock
4 ounces shelled fresh or frozen
   fava beans
2 tablespoons chopped fresh parsley
salt and ground black pepper

1 Heat 2 tablespoons of the oil in a large frying pan. Add half the meat and brown well on all sides. Transfer to a plate. Brown the rest of the meat in the same way and remove from the pan.

2 Heat the remaining oil in a large saucepan, add the onion and cook for about 5 minutes, until soft. Add the meat and mix well.

3 Add the garlic cloves, bay leaf, paprika and stock. Season with salt and pepper. Bring to a boil, then cover and simmer very gently for 1½–2 hours, until the meat is tender.

4 Add the fava beans about 10 minutes before the end of the cooking time. Stir in the parsley just before serving.

— NUTRITION NOTES —

Per portion:

Calories	414
Protein	53.1g
Fat	27g
Saturated fat	11.3g
Carbohydrate	3.1g
Sugar	1.1g
Fiber (NSP)	1.5g
Calcium	26mg

— COOK'S TIP —

Any canned beans such as navy or cannellini beans can be used instead of fava beans.

Turkish Lamb Pilaf

INGREDIENTS

Serves 4

3 tablespoons vegetable oil
1 large onion, finely chopped
1 pound lamb fillet, cut into
  small cubes
½ teaspoon ground cinnamon
2 tablespoons tomato paste
3 tablespoons chopped fresh parsley
½ cup dried apricots, halved
1 pound long-grain rice, rinsed
¾ cup pistachios, chopped (optional)
salt and ground black pepper
flat-leaf parsley, to garnish

1 Heat the oil in a large heavy pan. Add the onion and cook until golden. Add the lamb and brown on all sides, then stir in the cinnamon, salt and pepper. Cover and cook gently for 10 minutes.

2 Add the tomato paste and enough water to cover the meat. Stir in the parsley, then bring to a boil. Cover the pan and simmer very gently for 1½ hours, until the meat is tender.

3 Add enough water to the pan so you have about 2½ cups liquid. Add the apricots and rice and stir in the pistachios, if using.

4 Bring to a boil, cover tightly and simmer for about 20 minutes, until the rice is cooked. (You may have to add a little more water, if necessary.) Transfer to a warmed serving dish and garnish with parsley before serving.

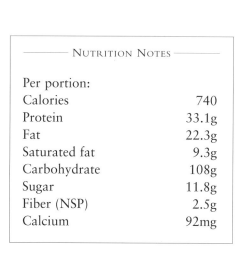

— NUTRITION NOTES —	
Per portion:	
Calories	740
Protein	33.1g
Fat	22.3g
Saturated fat	9.3g
Carbohydrate	108g
Sugar	11.8g
Fiber (NSP)	2.5g
Calcium	92mg

Pork-stuffed Cabbage Parcels

Served with rice, these attractive, tied parcels make a tasty meal.

INGREDIENTS

Serves 4

4 dried Chinese mushrooms, soaked in
 hot water until soft
2 ounces cellophane noodles, soaked in
 hot water until soft
1 pound ground pork
4 scallions, finely chopped, plus
 4 scallions to tie the parcels
2 garlic cloves, finely chopped
2 tablespoons fish sauce
12 large green cabbage leaves
2 tablespoons vegetable oil
1 small onion, finely chopped
2 garlic cloves, crushed
14-ounce can plum tomatoes
pinch of sugar
salt and ground black pepper

1 Drain the mushrooms, remove and discard the stems and coarsely chop the caps. Put them in a bowl.

2 Drain the noodles and cut them into short lengths. Add the noodles to the bowl with the pork, chopped scallions and garlic. Season with the fish sauce and add pepper to taste.

3 Cut off the stem from each cabbage leaf. Blanch the leaves in batches in a saucepan of boiling salted water for about 1 minute. Remove from the pan and refresh under cold water. Drain and dry on paper towels. Add the whole scallions to the boiling water and blanch in the same fashion. Drain well.

4 Fill one of the cabbage leaves with a generous spoonful of the pork and noodle filling. Roll up the leaf sufficiently to enclose the filling, then tuck in the sides and continue rolling the leaf to make a tight parcel. Make more parcels in the same way.

5 Split each blanched scallion lengthwise into three strands by cutting through the bulb and tearing upwards. Tie each of the cabbage parcels with a length of scallion.

6 Heat the oil in a large flameproof casserole. Add the onion and garlic and sauté for 2 minutes or until soft.

7 In a bowl, mash the tomatoes in their juice with a fork, then stir into the casserole. Season with salt, pepper and a pinch of sugar, then bring to a simmer. Add the cabbage parcels, cover and cook gently for 20–25 minutes or until the filling is cooked. Add a little water if the sauce is too dry.

NUTRITION NOTES	
Per portion:	
Calories	309
Protein	26.5g
Fat	13.9g
Saturated fat	3.4g
Carbohydrate	19.4g
Sugar	5.3g
Fiber (NSP)	2.2g
Calcium	60mg

Pork Tenderloin with Sage and Orange

Sage is often partnered with pork—there seems to be a natural affinity. The addition of orange brings complexity and balances the sometimes overpowering flavor of sage.

INGREDIENTS

Serves 4
2 pork tenderloins, about
   12 ounces each
1 tablespoon margarine
1¼ cups well-flavored chicken stock
2 garlic cloves, very finely chopped
grated zest and juice of
   1 unwaxed orange
3 or 4 sage leaves, finely chopped
2 teaspoons cornstarch or arrowroot
salt and ground black pepper
orange wedges and sage leaves,
   to garnish

1 Season the pork lightly with salt and pepper. Melt the margarine in a heavy flameproof casserole over medium-high heat, then add the meat and cook for 5–6 minutes, turning to brown all sides evenly.

2 Add the stock, boil for about 1 minute, then add the garlic, orange zest and sage. Bring to a boil; reduce the heat to low, then cover and simmer for 20 minutes, turning once, until the meat can be pierced with a knife. Transfer the pork to a warmed platter; cover.

3 Bring the sauce to a boil. Blend the cornstarch or arrowroot and orange juice and stir into the sauce, then boil gently over medium heat for a few minutes, stirring frequently, until the sauce is slightly thickened. Strain into a gravy boat or serving bowl.

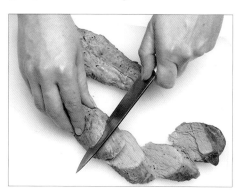

4 Slice the pork diagonally and pour the meat juices into the sauce.

5 Arrange the pork slices on warmed plates and spoon a little sauce over the top. Garnish with orange wedges and sage leaves and serve the remaining sauce separately.

NUTRITION NOTES	
Per portion:	
Calories	330
Protein	36.2g
Fat	15.5g
Saturated fat	5.7g
Carbohydrate	2.65g
Sugar	0.3g
Fiber (NSP)	0g
Calcium	16.7mg

Beef Rolls with Garlic and Tomato Sauce

Thin slices of beef are wrapped around a richly flavored stuffing in this classic Italian recipe.

INGREDIENTS

Serves 4

4 thin slices of round steak, about
    4 ounces each
4 slices smoked ham
1⅔ cups freshly grated Parmesan cheese
2 garlic cloves, crushed
5 tablespoons chopped fresh parsley
2 eggs, soft-boiled, shelled and
    chopped (optional)
3 tablespoons olive oil
1 large onion, finely chopped
⅔ cup tomato sauce
2 bay leaves
scant 1 cup beef stock
salt and ground black pepper
flat-leaf parsley, to garnish

1 Preheat the oven to 325°F. Place the beef slices on a sheet of waxed paper. Cover the beef with another sheet of waxed paper or plastic wrap and beat with a mallet or rolling pin until very thin. Place a ham slice over each.

2 Mix the cheese in a bowl with the garlic, parsley, eggs if using, and a little salt and pepper. Stir well until all the ingredients are evenly mixed.

3 Spoon the stuffing onto the ham and beef slices. Fold two opposite sides of the meat over the stuffing, then roll up the meat to form neat parcels. Secure with string.

4 Heat the oil in a frying pan. Add the parcels and brown quickly on all sides. Transfer to an ovenproof dish.

5 Add the onion to the frying pan and fry for 3 minutes. Stir in the tomato sauce, bay leaves and stock and season with salt and pepper. Bring to a boil, then pour the sauce over the meat in the dish.

6 Cover the dish and bake for 1 hour. Lift the beef rolls out of the pan using a slotted spoon and remove the string. Transfer to warm serving plates.

7 Taste the sauce, season with salt and pepper if necessary, and spoon it over the meat. Serve garnished with flat-leaf parsley.

NUTRITION NOTES

Per portion:

Calories	490
Protein	53.5g
Fat	28.1g
Saturated fat	12g
Carbohydrate	2.9g
Sugar	2.3g
Fiber (NSP)	0.6g
Calcium	470mg

FREE FROM

Spiced Grilled Poussins

The spice coating keeps the poussins moist as well as giving them a delicious flavor.

INGREDIENTS

Serves 4
2 garlic cloves, roughly chopped
1 teaspoon ground cumin
1 teaspoon ground coriander
pinch of cayenne pepper
½ small onion, chopped
¼ cup olive oil
½ teaspoon salt
2 poussins
lemon wedges, to garnish

VARIATION

Chicken pieces and lamb chops can also be cooked in this way.

---

1 Combine the garlic, cumin, coriander, cayenne pepper, onion, olive oil and salt in a food processor. Process to make a paste that will spread smoothly.

2 Cut the poussins in half lengthwise. Place them skin-side up in a shallow dish and spread with the spice paste. Cover and let marinate in a cool place for 2 hours.

3 Broil or grill the poussins for 15–20 minutes, turning them frequently, until cooked and lightly charred on the outside. Serve immediately, garnished with lemon wedges.

NUTRITION NOTES

Per portion:
Calories	239
Protein	23.1g
Fat	16.1g
Saturated fat	3.1g
Carbohydrate	0.6g
Sugar	0.4g
Fiber (NSP)	0.1g
Calcium	11mg

Chicken with Forty Cloves of Garlic

This recipe is not as strong-tasting as it sounds. Long, slow cooking makes the garlic soft and fragrant and the delicate flavor permeates the chicken.

INGREDIENTS

Serves 4
½ lemon
fresh rosemary sprigs
3 pound chicken
4 garlic bulbs
¼ cup olive oil
salt and ground black pepper
steamed fava beans and scallions,
    to serve

1 Preheat the oven to 375°F. Place the lemon and rosemary in the chicken. Separate three of the garlic bulbs into cloves and remove the husks, but do not peel. Slice the top off the other garlic bulb.

2 Heat the oil in a large flameproof casserole. Add the chicken, turning it in the oil to coat. Season with salt and pepper and add all the garlic.

3 Cover the casserole with foil, then the lid, to seal well. Cook in the oven for 1–1¼ hours, until the chicken is tender. Remove the chicken and whole garlic from the casserole. Mash the remaining garlic into the pan juices to make a sauce and serve the chicken with the roast garlic and the garlic sauce, accompanied by steamed fava beans and scallions.

NUTRITION NOTES

Per portion:
Calories	354
Protein	69.7g
Fat	26.2g
Saturated fat	5.9g
Carbohydrate	4.9g
Sugar	0.5g
Fiber (NSP)	1.23g
Calcium	32mg

Mediterranean Roasted Chicken

This is a delicious alternative to a traditional roast chicken. Use a corn-fed or free-range bird, if available, and choose organic vegetables. This recipe also works well with guinea fowl.

INGREDIENTS

Serves 4
4–4½ pound roasting chicken
⅔ cup extra virgin olive oil
½ lemon
few sprigs of fresh thyme
1 pound small new potatoes
1 eggplant, cut into 1-inch cubes
1 red bell pepper, seeded and quartered
1 fennel bulb, trimmed and quartered
8 large garlic cloves, unpeeled
coarse salt and ground black pepper

3 Remove the chicken from the oven and season with salt. Turn the chicken breast-side up, and baste with the juices from the pan.

4 Surround the bird with the new potatoes, roll the potatoes in the pan juices until coated, return the pan to the oven, and continue roasting for 30 minutes.

7 To find out if the chicken is cooked, push the tip of a sharp knife between the thigh and breast. If the juices run clear, it is done. If not, return the chicken to the oven for about 10 minutes more and test again. The vegetables should be tender and just beginning to brown.

8 Serve the chicken and vegetables from the pan, or transfer the vegetables to a serving dish, carve the chicken and place it on top. Serve the skimmed juices in a gravy boat.

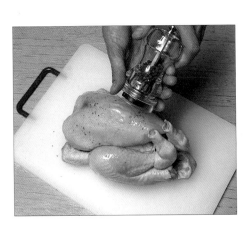

1 Preheat the oven to 400°F. Rub the chicken all over with some of the extra-virgin olive oil and season with pepper.

2 Place the lemon half inside the bird, with a sprig or two of thyme. Put the chicken breast-side down in a large roasting pan. Transfer to the oven and roast for about 30 minutes.

5 Remove the pan from the oven and add the eggplant, red pepper, fennel and garlic cloves. Drizzle with the remaining olive oil and season with salt and pepper.

6 Add any remaining thyme to the vegetables. Return the pan to the oven and cook for 30–50 minutes more, basting and turning the vegetables occasionally.

---— COOK'S TIP —---

Extra-virgin olive oil is the highest quality, obtained by a single cold pressing of the finest olives. It has a pure fruity flavor which makes it ideal for cooking.

---— NUTRITION NOTES —---

Per portion:
Calories	724
Protein	70g
Fat	40g
Saturated fat	8.1g
Carbohydrate	22.2g
Sugar	5.4g
Fiber (NSP)	3.72g
Calcium	52mg

Stoved Chicken

In great Britain, "stovies" are potatoes slowly cooked on the stove with onions and meat juices or butter until falling to pieces. This version includes a succulent layer of bacon and chicken in the middle.

INGREDIENTS

Serves 4

2¼ pounds baking potatoes, cut into ¼-inch slices
2 large onions, thinly sliced
1 tablespoon chopped fresh thyme
2 tablespoons butter
1 tablespoon vegetable oil
2 large bacon slices, chopped
4 large chicken pieces, halved
2½ cups chicken stock
1 bay leaf
salt and ground black pepper

1 Preheat the oven to 300°F. Arrange a thick layer of half the potato slices in the bottom of a large baking dish, then cover with half the onions. Sprinkle with half of the thyme, and season.

2 Heat the butter and oil in a large heavy frying pan, add the bacon and chicken and brown on all sides. Using a slotted spoon, transfer the chicken and bacon to the baking dish. Reserve the fat in the pan.

3 Sprinkle the remaining thyme over the chicken, season with salt and pepper, then cover with the remaining onions, followed by a neat layer of overlapping potato slices. Season well.

4 Pour the stock over the potatoes. Tuck in the bay leaf and brush the potatoes with the reserved fat. Cover and bake for 1–1½ hours, until the chicken is tender.

5 Preheat the broiler. Uncover the baking dish and broil until the potato is brown and crisp. Remove the bay leaf and serve hot.

— NUTRITION NOTES —	
Per portion:	
Calories	565
Protein	47g
Fat	22.5g
Saturated fat	8.7g
Carbohydrate	45g
Sugar	3.1g
Fiber (NSP)	3.7g
Calcium	37mg

Spiced Duck with Pears

This delicious casserole is based on a Catalan dish that uses goose or duck. The sautéed pears are added toward the end of cooking, along with picarda sauce, a pounded pine nut and garlic paste that both flavors and thickens.

INGREDIENTS

Serves 6

6 duck pieces, either breast or
   leg pieces
1 tablespoon olive oil
1 large onion, thinly sliced
1 cinnamon stick, halved
2 thyme sprigs
2 cups chicken stock

To finish

3 firm ripe pears
2 tablespoons olive oil
2 garlic cloves, sliced
⅓ cup pine nuts
½ teaspoon saffron strands
2 tablespoons raisins
salt and ground black pepper
thyme sprigs or fresh parsley,
   to garnish
mashed potato and a green vegetable
   (optional), to serve

1 Preheat the oven to 350°F. Brown the duck portions in the olive oil for about 5 minutes until the skin is golden. Transfer the duck to an ovenproof dish and drain off all but 1 tablespoon of the fat left in the pan.

2 Add the onion to the pan and sauté, stirring, for 5 minutes. Add the cinnamon stick, thyme and stock and bring to a boil. Pour over the duck and bake for 1¼ hours.

3 Meanwhile, peel, core and halve the pears and sauté in the oil until beginning to turn golden on the cut sides. Pound the garlic, pine nuts and saffron in a mortar, with a pestle, to make a thick, smooth paste.

4 Add the garlic and pine nut paste to the casserole along with the raisins and pears. Return the dish to the oven and bake for another 15 minutes, until the pears are tender.

5 Season to taste with salt and pepper and garnish with parsley or thyme. Serve with mashed potatoes and a green vegetable, if desired.

NUTRITION NOTES	
Per portion:	
Calories	783
Protein	56.5g
Fat	35.7g
Saturated fat	8.3g
Carbohydrate	51.3g
Sugar	57.2g
Fiber (NSP)	7.8g
Calcium	103mg

FREE FROM

FISH AND SHELLFISH

Explore some of the world's cuisines with the fish recipes in this

chapter. From France you can sample Mediterranean Baked Fish;

from Italy you have Fresh Tuna and Tomato Stew. From farther

afield, you can try Fish Balls with Chinese Greens and, still in an

Asian mood, there's an Indonesian speciality, Spiced Shrimp with

Coconut. All these recipes combine wonderful taste sensations

and bring you delicious and healthy dishes.

Mediterranean Baked Fish

INGREDIENTS

Serves 4

3 potatoes
2 tablespoons extra-virgin olive oil,
    plus extra for drizzling
2 onions, halved and sliced
2 garlic cloves, very finely chopped
1½ pounds thick skinless fish fillets,
    such as turbot or sea bass
1 bay leaf
1 thyme sprig
3 tomatoes, peeled and thinly sliced
2 tablespoons orange juice
¼ cup fish stock
½ teaspoon saffron threads, steeped in
    ¼ cup boiling water
salt and ground black pepper

1 Cook the potatoes in boiling salted water for 15 minutes, then drain and let cool. When the potatoes are cool enough to handle, peel off the skins and slice them thinly.

NUTRITION NOTES

Per portion:

Calories	300
Protein	32.2g
Fat	10.4g
Saturated fat	2.03g
Carbohydrate	17.9g
Sugar	4.7g
Fiber (NSP)	2.1g
Calcium	100mg

2 Meanwhile, heat the olive oil in a heavy frying pan and sauté the onions over medium-low heat for about 10 minutes, stirring frequently. Add the garlic and continue cooking for a few minutes, until the onions are soft and golden.

3 Preheat the oven to 375°F. Layer half the potato slices in an 8-cup baking dish. Cover with half the onions. Season with salt and pepper.

4 Place the fish fillets on top of the vegetables and tuck the herbs in between them. Top with the tomato slices and then the remaining onions and potatoes.

5 Pour the orange juice, stock and saffron liquid over, season with salt and pepper and drizzle a little extra olive oil on top. Bake, uncovered, for about 30 minutes, until the potatoes are tender and the fish is cooked.

Fish with Spinach and Lime

The fish is marinated in a fragrant herb marinade called a *charmoula* in Middle Eastern cooking.

INGREDIENTS

Serves 4

1½ pounds white fish, such as haddock, cod, sea bass or monkfish
sunflower oil, for frying
1¼ pounds potatoes, sliced
1 onion, chopped
1–2 garlic cloves, crushed
5 tomatoes, peeled and chopped
12 ounces fresh spinach, chopped
lime wedges, to garnish

For the *charmoula*

6 scallions, chopped
2 teaspoons fresh thyme
¼ cup chopped flat-leaf parsley
2 tablespoons chopped cilantro
2 teaspoons paprika
generous pinch of cayenne pepper
¼ cup olive oil
grated zest of 1 lime and ¼ cup
    lime juice
salt

1 Cut the fish into large pieces, discarding any skin and bones, and place in a large shallow dish.

2 Blend together the ingredients for the *charmoula* and season well with salt. Pour over the fish, stir to mix and let sit in a cool place, covered with plastic wrap, for 2–4 hours.

3 Heat about ¼ inch oil in a large heavy pan and fry the potatoes until cooked through and golden. Drain on paper towels.

4 Pour off all but about 1 tablespoon of the oil and add the chopped onion, garlic and tomatoes. Cook over low heat for 5–6 minutes, stirring occasionally, until the onion is soft.

5 Place the potatoes on top of the onion and tomato mixture, then add the chopped spinach to the pan.

6 Place the fish on top of the spinach and pour in all the marinade. Cover tightly and cook for 15–18 minutes. After about 8 minutes, carefully stir the contents of the pan so that the fish is distributed evenly throughout the dish. Cover the pan again and continue cooking, but check occasionally—the dish is cooked once the fish is tender and opaque and the spinach has wilted.

7 Serve immediately on individual serving plates, garnished with wedges of lime.

NUTRITION NOTES

Per portion:	
Calories	369
Protein	36.5g
Fat	13.6g
Saturated fat	2.06g
Carbohydrate	26.3g
Sugar	7.4g
Fiber (NSP)	4.5g
Calcium	174mg

Fish Balls with Chinese Greens

Tasty fish balls are partnered with a selection of green vegetables to make a fresh and appetizing stir-fry with a Chinese flavor.

INGREDIENTS

Serves 4

1 pound white fish fillets, skinned, boned and cubed
3 scallions, chopped
1 slice bacon, chopped
1 tablespoon Chinese rice wine
2 tablespoons tamari
1 egg white

For the vegetables

1 teaspoon cornstarch or arrowroot
1 tablespoon tamari
⅔ cup fish stock
2 tablespoons vegetable oil
2 garlic cloves, sliced
1-inch piece fresh ginger, cut into thin shreds
3 ounces green beans
6 ounces snow peas
3 scallions, sliced diagonally into 2–3 inch lengths
1 small head bok choy, stems trimmed and leaves torn
salt and ground black pepper

--- COOK'S TIP ---

Tamari is a wheat-free type of soy sauce and can be found at Asian stores. If you are not allergic to wheat, you can substitute soy sauce, if you prefer.

--- NUTRITION NOTES ---

Per portion:
Calories	201
Protein	26.5g
Fat	8.75g
Saturated fat	1.5g
Carbohydrate	3.9g
Sugar	3.2g
Fiber (NSP)	2.2g
Calcium	67mg

1 Put the fish, scallions, bacon, rice wine, tamari and egg white in a food processor. Process until smooth. With wetted hands, form the mixture into about 24 small balls.

2 Steam the fish balls in batches in a lightly greased bamboo steamer in a wok for 5–10 minutes, until firm. Transfer to a plate and keep warm.

3 In a small bowl, blend together the cornstarch or arrowroot, tamari and stock until smooth. Set aside.

4 Heat a wok until hot, add the oil and swirl it around. Add the garlic and ginger and stir-fry for 1 minute. Add the beans and stir-fry for 2–3 minutes, then add the snow peas, scallions and bok choy. Stir-fry for 2–3 minutes.

5 Add the stock mixture to the wok and cook, stirring, until it has thickened and the vegetables are tender but still crisp. Taste, and adjust the seasoning if necessary. Serve at once with the steamed fish balls.

Tuna with Pan-fried Tomatoes

INGREDIENTS

Serves 2

2 tuna steaks, about 6 ounces each
6 tablespoons olive oil
2 tablespoons lemon juice
2 garlic cloves, chopped
1 teaspoon chopped fresh thyme
4 canned anchovy fillets, drained and
  finely chopped
8 ounces plum tomatoes, halved
2 tablespoons chopped fresh parsley
4–6 black olives, pitted and chopped
ground black pepper
crusty bread, to serve (optional)

3 Meanwhile, heat the remaining oil in a frying pan. Add the tomatoes and sauté for 2 minutes on each side.

4 Divide the tomatoes equally between two serving plates and scatter the chopped parsley and olives over. Top each with a tuna steak.

5 Add the remaining marinade to the pan juices and warm through. Pour over the tomatoes and tuna steaks and serve immediately with bread (if your diet allows) for mopping up the juices.

NUTRITION NOTES	
Per portion:	
Calories	578
Protein	21.8g
Fat	21.6g
Saturated fat	7.2g
Carbohydrate	3.6g
Sugar	3.6g
Fiber (NSP)	1.4g
Calcium	57mg

1 Place the tuna steaks in a shallow nonmetallic dish. Mix 4 tablespoons of the oil with the lemon juice, garlic, thyme, anchovies and pepper. Pour this mixture over the tuna and set aside to marinate in a cool place for at least 1 hour.

2 Lift the tuna from the marinade and place on a broiler rack. Broil for 4 minutes on each side, or until firm to the touch, basting with the marinade. Take care not to overcook.

Red Snapper with Cumin

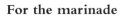
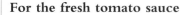

INGREDIENTS

Serves 4

8–12 small red snapper, depending on the size of the fish
fresh parsley and finely pared strips of lemon zest, to garnish

For the marinade
2 teaspoons ground cumin
1 teaspoon paprika
¼ cup lemon juice
3 tablespoons olive oil
2 tablespoons chopped fresh parsley
salt and ground black pepper

For the fresh tomato sauce
5 large tomatoes
2 garlic cloves, chopped
¼ cup chopped fresh parsley and cilantro
2 tablespoons olive oil
2 tablespoons lemon juice

1 Make 2–3 slashes along the sides of the fish and place them in a shallow nonmetallic dish. Blend together the ingredients for the marinade and rub into the fish on both sides. Set aside for 2 hours in a cool place.

2 Make the fresh tomato sauce. Peel the tomatoes and cut into small pieces, discarding the core and seeds. Place in a bowl and stir in the remaining ingredients. Set aside in the refrigerator or a cool place.

3 Heat the broiler or prepare the barbecue. Broil or grill the fish for 3–4 minutes on each side, until the flesh is tender. Garnish with parsley and lemon zest and serve immediately with the fresh tomato sauce.

NUTRITION NOTES	
Per portion:	
Calories	334
Protein	33.1g
Fat	21.1g
Saturated fat	2.1g
Carbohydrate	3.65g
Sugar	3.65g
Fiber (NSP)	1.1g
Calcium	130mg

Spicy Fish Brochettes

INGREDIENTS

Serves 4 as an appetizer

1 pound white fish fillets, such as cod, haddock, monkfish or sea bass
olive oil, for brushing
lime wedges and fresh tomato sauce, to serve

For the spicy marinade
½ onion, grated or very finely chopped
2 garlic cloves, crushed
2 tablespoons chopped fresh cilantro
1 tablespoon chopped fresh parsley
1 teaspoon ground cumin
2 teaspoons paprika
good pinch of ground ginger
1½ tablespoons white wine vinegar
2 tablespoons lime juice
salt and cayenne pepper

1 First make the marinade. Blend all the ingredients and season to taste with salt and cayenne pepper.

2 Cut the fish into ½-inch cubes, discarding the skin and bones. Place in a shallow nonmetallic dish. Add the marinade and stir to coat the fish thoroughly. Cover with plastic wrap and set aside for about 2 hours.

3 Preheat the broiler. Thread the fish on to 12 small or 8 larger metal skewers. Place on a broiler pan and brush with a little olive oil. Cook the brochettes for 7–10 minutes until the fish is cooked through, turning and brushing with more oil occasionally.

NUTRITION NOTES	
Per portion:	
Calories	77
Protein	17.7g
Fat	0.4g
Saturated fat	0.1g
Carbohydrate	0.7g
Sugar	0.5g
Fiber (NSP)	0.1g
Calcium	11mg

Halibut with Tomato Vinaigrette

The tomato vinaigrette, an uncooked mixture of tomatoes, aromatic fresh herbs and olive oil, can either be served at room temperature or slightly warm.

INGREDIENTS

Serves 2

3 large ripe beefsteak tomatoes, peeled, seeded and chopped
2 shallots or 1 small red onion, finely chopped
1 garlic clove, crushed
6 tablespoons chopped mixed fresh herbs, such as parsley, cilantro, basil, tarragon, chervil or chives
½ cup extra-virgin olive oil, plus extra for brushing
4 halibut fillets or steaks, about 6–7 ounces each
salt and ground black pepper
green salad, to serve

1 In a medium bowl, combine the tomatoes, shallots or onion, garlic and herbs. Stir in the oil and season with salt and ground pepper. Cover the bowl and leave the sauce at room temperature for about 1 hour to let the flavors blend.

2 Preheat the broiler. Line a broiler pan with foil and brush the foil lightly with oil.

3 Season the fish with salt and pepper. Place the fish on the foil and brush with a little extra oil. Broil the fish for 5–6 minutes, until the flesh is opaque and the top is lightly browned.

4 Pour the tomato vinaigrette into a saucepan and heat gently for a few minutes. Serve the fish with the sauce and a green salad.

NUTRITION NOTES	
Per portion:	
Calories	652
Protein	44.5g
Fat	49.5g
Saturated fat	7.3g
Carbohydrate	7.2g
Sugar	6.6g
Fiber (NSP)	1.9g
Calcium	90.5mg

Fresh Tuna and Tomato Stew

This tuna stew has a delicious Italian flavor.

INGREDIENTS

Serves 4

12 pearl onions, peeled
2 pounds ripe tomatoes
1½ pounds fresh tuna
3 tablespoons olive oil
2 garlic cloves, crushed
3 tablespoons chopped fresh herbs
2 bay leaves
½ teaspoon sugar
2 tablespoons sun-dried tomato paste
⅔ cup fish stock
salt and ground black pepper
baby zucchini and fresh herbs,
    to garnish

1 Leave the onions whole and cook in a pan of boiling water for 4–5 minutes, until softened. Drain.

2 Plunge the tomatoes into boiling water for 30 seconds, then rinse in cold water. Peel away the skins and chop the tomatoes roughly.

3 Cut the tuna into 1-inch chunks. Heat the oil in a large frying or sauté pan and quickly fry the tuna until browned. Transfer the tuna chunks to paper towels to drain.

4 Add the onions, garlic, tomatoes, chopped herbs, bay leaves, sugar, tomato paste and stock and bring to a boil, breaking up the tomatoes with a wooden spoon.

5 Reduce the heat and simmer gently for 5 minutes. Return the fish to the sauce in the pan and cook for another 5 minutes. Season, and serve hot, garnished with baby zucchini and fresh herbs.

----- COOK'S TIP -----

The best fresh herbs to use as a garnish for tuna are basil, parsley or chives.

----- NUTRITION NOTES -----

Per portion:

Calories	412
Protein	42.5g
Fat	18.7g
Saturated fat	3.7g
Carbohydrate	13.1g
Sugar	11.3g
Fiber (NSP)	3.3g
Calcium	66mg

FREE FROM

Buckwheat Noodles with Smoked Trout

These earthy flavors mix perfectly with the crisp bok choy.

INGREDIENTS

Serves 4

12 ounces buckwheat noodles
2 tablespoons vegetable oil
4 ounces fresh shiitake
    mushrooms, quartered
2 garlic cloves, finely chopped
1 tablespoon grated fresh ginger
8 ounces bok choy
1 scallion, finely sliced diagonally
1 tablespoon dark sesame oil
2 tablespoons mirin
2 tablespoons tamari or soy sauce
2 smoked trout, skinned and boned
salt and ground back pepper
2 tablespoons cilantro leaves and
    2 teaspoons sesame seeds, toasted,
    to garnish (optional)

1 Cook the buckwheat noodles in boiling water for 7–10 minutes, until just tender or according to the package instructions.

2 Meanwhile, heat the oil in a large frying pan. Add the mushrooms and cook, stirring, over a medium heat for 3 minutes. Add the garlic, ginger and bok choy, and continue to cook for 2 minutes.

3 Drain the noodles and add them to the mushroom mixture with the scallion, sesame oil, mirin and tamari. Toss and season with salt and pepper to taste.

4 Break the smoked trout into bite-size pieces. Arrange the noodle mixture on individual serving plates. Place the smoked trout on top of the noodles.

5 Garnish the noodles with cilantro leaves and sesame seeds, if you wish, and serve them immediately.

NUTRITION NOTES	
Per portion:	
Calories	513
Protein	27.2g
Fat	16.7g
Saturated fat	1.5g
Carbohydrate	67.2g
Sugar	2.9g
Fiber (NSP)	3.5g
Calcium	65mg

Spiced Shrimp with Coconut

This delicious, fragrant and spicy dish is based on a traditional Indonesian recipe. Serve with a bowl of plain boiled rice.

INGREDIENTS

Serves 3–4

2–3 fresh red chiles, seeded and chopped
3 shallots, chopped
1 lemongrass stalk, chopped
2 garlic cloves, chopped
thin sliver of dried shrimp paste
½ teaspoon ground ginger
1 teaspoon ground turmeric
1 teaspoon ground coriander
1 tablespoon vegetable oil
1 cup water
2 fresh kaffir lime leaves
1 teaspoon light brown sugar
2 tomatoes, peeled, seeded and chopped
1 cup coconut milk
1½ pounds large raw shrimp, peeled and deveined
squeeze of lemon juice
salt, to taste
shredded scallions and toasted shredded coconut, to garnish

1 In a mortar, pound the chiles, shallots, lemongrass, garlic, shrimp paste, ginger, turmeric and coriander with a pestle until it forms a paste. Alternatively, process the ingredients in a food processor or blender.

NUTRITION NOTES

Per portion:

Calories	184–246
Protein	30–40g
Fat	4.2–5.4g
Saturated fat	0.6–0.8g
Carbohydrate	6.9–9.3g
Sugar	6.3–8.8g
Fiber (NSP)	0.7–0.9g
Calcium	159–212mg

2 Heat a wok until hot, add the oil and swirl it around. Add the spiced paste and stir-fry for about 2 minutes. Pour in the water and add the kaffir lime leaves, sugar and tomatoes. Simmer for 8–10 minutes, until most of the liquid has evaporated.

3 Add the coconut milk and shrimp and cook gently, stirring, for about 4 minutes until the shrimp are pink. Taste and adjust the seasoning with salt and a squeeze of lemon juice. Serve immediately, garnished with shredded scallions and toasted coconut.

FREE FROM

VEGETABLES AND VEGETARIAN DISHES

Fresh vegetables are a vital part of an allergy-free diet, and here you will find a selection of recipes using seasonal vegetables to their best advantage. Delicious ideas include Middle Eastern Vegetable Stew, Ratatouille and Roasted Vegetable Salad. Baby vegetables make a delicious accompaniment in Braised Summer Vegetables, and seasonal peas and beans enhance Risotto with Spring Vegetables.

Braised Summer Vegetables

FREE FROM

Tender, young vegetables are ideal for quick cooking in a minimum of liquid. Use any mixture of your favorite vegetables as long as they are of similar size.

INGREDIENTS

Serves 4
2½ cups baby carrots
2 cups sugar-snap peas
   or snow peas
4 ounces baby corn
6 tablespoons vegetable stock
2 teaspoons lime juice
salt and ground black pepper
chopped fresh parsley and snipped fresh
   chives, to garnish

3 Season the vegetables with salt and pepper to taste, then add the parsley and chives.

4 Cook the vegetables for a few more seconds, stirring them once or twice, until the herbs are well mixed, then serve immediately.

— COOK'S TIP —
You can make this dish in the winter, too, but cut larger, tougher vegetables into chunks and cook for slightly longer.

— NUTRITION NOTES —

Per portion:
Calories	34
Protein	2.6g
Fat	0.4g
Saturated fat	0g
Carbohydrate	5.2g
Sugar	4.4g
Fiber (NSP)	2.6g
Calcium	38.7mg

1 Place the carrots, peas and baby corn in a large, heavy saucepan with the vegetable stock and lime juice. Bring to a boil.

2 Cover the pan and reduce the heat, then simmer for 6–8 minutes, shaking the pan occasionally, until the vegetables are just tender.

Middle Eastern Vegetable Stew

A spicy dish of mixed vegetables that can be served as a side dish or as a main course. Children may prefer less chili powder.

INGREDIENTS

Serves 4–6
3 tablespoons vegetable or chicken stock
1 green bell pepper, seeded and sliced
2 zucchini, sliced
2 carrots, sliced
2 celery stalks, sliced
2 potatoes, diced
14-ounce can chopped tomatoes
1 teaspoon chili powder
2 tablespoons chopped fresh mint
1 tablespoon ground cumin
14-ounce can chickpeas, drained
salt and ground black pepper
mint leaves, to garnish

1 Heat the stock in a large flameproof casserole until boiling, then add the sliced pepper, zucchini, carrots and celery. Stir over a high heat for 2–3 minutes, until the vegetables are just beginning to soften.

NUTRITION NOTES	
Per portion:	
Calories	141–212
Protein	7.5–11.2g
Fat	2.4–3.6g
Saturated fat	0.3–0.4g
Carbohydrate	23.8–35.7g
Sugar	4.8–7.2g
Fiber(NSP)	5.1–7.7g
Calcium	60.3–90.5mg

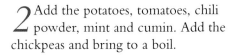

2 Add the potatoes, tomatoes, chili powder, mint and cumin. Add the chickpeas and bring to a boil.

—— COOK'S TIP ——

Chickpeas are traditional in this type of Middle Eastern dish but, if you prefer, red kidney beans or navy beans can be used instead.

3 Reduce the heat, cover the casserole with a lid and simmer for 30 minutes or until all the vegetables are tender.

4 Season the stew with salt and pepper to taste and serve hot, garnished with mint leaves.

FREE FROM

Ratatouille

FREE FROM

This classic combination of the vegetables that grow abundantly in the south of France is infinitely flexible. Use the recipe as a guide for making the most of what you have on hand.

INGREDIENTS

Serves 6

2 eggplant, about 1 pound total, cut into ¾-inch slices
4–5 tablespoons olive oil
1 large onion, halved and sliced
2 or 3 garlic cloves, very finely chopped
1 large red or yellow bell pepper, seeded and cut into thin strips
2 large zucchini, cut into ½-inch slices
1½ pounds ripe tomatoes, peeled, seeded and chopped, or 14-ounce can chopped tomatoes
1 teaspoon dried mixed herbs
salt and ground black pepper

COOK'S TIP

Roasting the pepper not only allows you to remove the skin, it adds a delicious, smoky flavor to the ratatouille. Quarter the pepper and broil, skin-side up, until blackened. Enclose the pepper in a sturdy plastic bag and set aside until cool. Peel off the skin, then remove the core and seeds and cut the pepper into strips. Add to the mixture with the cooked eggplant.

NUTRITION NOTES

Per portion:

Calories	95
Protein	1.9g
Fat	7.7g
Saturated fat	1.2g
Carbohydrate	7.4g
Sugar	4.3g
Fiber (NSP)	1.9g
Calcium	28mg

1 Preheat the broiler. Brush the eggplant slices with oil on both sides. Broil until lightly browned, turning once, then cut into chunks.

2 Heat 1 tablespoon of the olive oil in a large flameproof casserole and cook the onion for about 10 minutes until lightly golden, stirring frequently. Add the garlic, pepper and zucchini and cook for a further 10 minutes.

3 Add the tomatoes, eggplant, dried herbs and salt and pepper. Simmer gently, covered, over low heat for about 20 minutes, stirring occasionally. Uncover and continue cooking for another 20–25 minutes, stirring occasionally, until all the vegetables are tender and the cooking liquid has thickened slightly. Serve hot or at room temperature, if you prefer.

Risotto with Spring Vegetables

This is one of the prettiest risottos, especially if you can get summer squash.

INGREDIENTS

Serves 4

1 cup shelled fresh peas
1 cup green beans, cut into
    short lengths
2 tablespoons olive oil
6 tablespoons butter
2 small yellow summer squash, cut
    into matchsticks
1 onion, finely chopped
1½ cups risotto rice
½ cup Italian dry
    white vermouth (optional)
about 4 cups boiling chicken stock
1 cup grated Parmesan cheese
a small handful of fresh basil leaves,
    finely shredded, plus a few whole
    leaves, to garnish
salt and ground black pepper

1 Blanch the peas and beans in a large saucepan of lightly salted boiling water for 2–3 minutes, until just tender. Drain, refresh under cold running water, drain and set aside.

2 Heat the oil and 2 tablespoons of the butter in a medium saucepan until foaming. Add the squash and cook gently for 2–3 minutes, or until just softened. Remove the squash with a slotted spoon and set aside. Add the onion to the pan and cook gently for about 3 minutes, stirring frequently, until softened.

3 Stir in the rice until the grains start to swell and burst, then add the vermouth, if using. Stir until the vermouth stops sizzling and most of it has been absorbed by the rice, then add a few ladlefuls of the stock, with salt and pepper to taste. Stir over low heat until the stock has been absorbed.

4 Continue cooking and stirring for 20–25 minutes, adding the remaining stock a few ladlefuls at a time. The rice should be *al dente* and the risotto should have a moist and creamy appearance. Gently stir in the vegetables and the remaining butter.

5 Stir in half the Parmesan. Heat through, then stir in the shredded basil and taste for seasoning. Garnish with basil leaves and pass around the remaining Parmesan.

NUTRITION NOTES	
Per portion:	
Calories	602
Protein	17.2g
Fat	28.9g
Saturated fat	15g
Carbohydrate	59.3g
Sugar	3.9g
Fiber (NSP)	2.9g
Calcium	272mg

Stuffed Grape Leaves

A traditional Greek recipe that comes in many guises. This vegetarian version is richly flavored with fresh herbs, lemon and a little chile. Serve as an appetizer or vegetarian main course or as part of a buffet spread.

Ingredients

Serves 6

8 ounce package preserved grape
   leaves, drained
1 onion, finely chopped
½ bunch of scallions,
   finely chopped
¼ cup chopped fresh flat-leaf parsley
10 large mint sprigs, chopped
finely grated zest of 1 lemon
½ teaspoon crushed dried chiles
1½ teaspoons fennel seed, crushed
scant 1 cup long grain rice
½ cup extra-virgin olive oil
salt
lemon wedges and mint leaves, to
   garnish (optional)

1 Rinse the grape leaves in plenty of cold water. Put in a bowl, cover with boiling water and let stand for 10 minutes. Drain thoroughly.

2 In a bowl, combine the onion, scallions, parsley, mint, lemon zest, chile, fennel seed, rice and 1½ tablespoons of the olive oil. Mix thoroughly and season with salt.

3 Place a grape leaf, veined side facing upwards, on a work surface and cut off any stalk. Place a heaping teaspoonful of the rice mixture near the stalk end of the leaf.

4 Fold the stalk end of the leaf over the rice filling, then fold over the sides and carefully roll up into a neat cigar shape.

5 Repeat with the remaining filling to make about 28 stuffed leaves. If some of the grape leaves are quite small, use two and patch them together to make parcels of the same size.

6 Place any remaining leaves in the bottom of a large, heavy saucepan. Pack the stuffed leaves in a single layer in the pan. Spoon the remaining oil over, then add about 1¼ cups boiling water.

7 Place a small plate over the leaves to keep them submerged in the water. Cover the pan and cook over very low heat for 45 minutes.

8 Transfer the stuffed leaves to a serving plate and garnish with lemon wedges and mint, if desired.

Cook's Tip

To check that the rice is cooked, lift out one stuffed leaf and cut in half. The rice should have expanded and softened to make a firm parcel. If necessary, cook the stuffed leaves a little longer, adding boiling water if the pan is becoming dry.

Nutrition Notes

Per portion:

Calories	256
Protein	3.9g
Fat	15.8g
Saturated fat	2.3g
Carbohydrate	26.3g
Sugar	1.6g
Fiber (NSP)	0.5g
Calcium	170mg

Free From

Green Beans with Tomatoes

FREE FROM

This is a real summer favorite using the best ripe plum tomatoes and green beans.

INGREDIENTS

Serves 4

2 tablespoons olive oil
1 large onion, finely sliced
2 garlic cloves, finely chopped
6 large ripe plum tomatoes, peeled, seeded and coarsely chopped
⅔ cup vegetable stock
1 pound green beans, sliced in half lengthwise
16 pitted black olives
2 teaspoons lemon juice
salt and ground black pepper

1 Heat the oil in a large frying pan. Add the onion and garlic and cook for about 5 minutes, until softened.

2 Add the chopped tomatoes, stock, beans, olives and lemon juice, and cook over low heat for another 20 minutes, stirring occasionally, until the sauce is thickened and the beans are tender. Season with salt and pepper to taste and serve immediately.

COOK'S TIP

Green beans need little preparation and now that they are grown without the string you simply trim them. When buying make sure that the beans snap easily—this is a good sign of freshness.

NUTRITION NOTES

Per portion:

Calories	140
Protein	3.3g
Fat	7.7g
Saturated fat	1.2g
Carbohydrate	7.98g
Sugar	7.38g
Fiber (NSP)	4.3g
Calcium	63mg

Polenta with Mushroom Sauce

Polenta, made from corn, forms the starchy base for many Italian dishes. Its subtle taste works well with the rich mushroom sauce.

INGREDIENTS

Serves 4

5 cups vegetable stock
3 cups polenta
⅔ cup grated
   Parmesan cheese
salt and ground black pepper

For the sauce

1 cup dried porcini mushrooms
1 tablespoon olive oil
¼ cup margarine
1 onion, finely chopped
1 carrot, finely chopped
1 celery stalk, finely chopped
2 garlic cloves, crushed
6 cups mixed cremini and portobello
   mushrooms, roughly chopped
½ cup vegetable stock
14-ounce can chopped tomatoes
1 tablespoon tomato paste
1 tablespoon chopped fresh
   thyme leaves

1 Make the sauce. Put the dried mushrooms in a bowl, add ⅔ cup hot water and soak for 20 minutes. Drain the mushrooms, reserving the liquid, and chop them roughly.

2 Heat the oil and margarine in a saucepan and add the onion, carrot, celery and garlic. Cook over low heat for about 5 minutes until the vegetables are beginning to soften, then raise the heat and add the fresh and soaked dried mushrooms to the pan of vegetables. Cook for 8–10 minutes, until the mushrooms are softened and golden.

4 Meanwhile, heat the stock for the polenta in a large, heavy saucepan. Add a generous pinch of salt. As soon as it simmers, pour in the polenta in a fine stream, whisking until the mixture is smooth. Cook for 30 minutes, stirring constantly, until the polenta comes away from the pan. Remove from heat and stir in half the Parmesan and some black pepper.

3 Add the stock and boil for 2–3 minutes until reduced, then add the tomatoes and mushroom liquid. Stir in the tomato paste, thyme and salt and pepper. Lower the heat and simmer for 20 minutes, until the sauce is thickened.

5 Divide the cooked polenta among four heated bowls and top each with the mushroom sauce. Sprinkle with the remaining Parmesan and serve immediately.

NUTRITION NOTES	
Per portion:	
Calories	550
Protein	17.2g
Fat	21.3g
Saturated fat	7.6g
Carbohydrate	68.4g
Sugar	5g
Fiber (NSP)	3.1g
Calcium	201mg

FREE FROM

Cauliflower with Tomatoes and Cumin

This makes an excellent side dish to serve with grilled or broiled meat or fish.

INGREDIENTS

Serves 4
2 tablespoons sunflower or olive oil
1 onion, chopped
1 garlic clove, crushed
1 small cauliflower, broken into florets
1 teaspoon cumin seeds
a good pinch of ground ginger
4 tomatoes, peeled, seeded
    and quartered
1–2 tablespoons lemon
    juice (optional)
2 tablespoons chopped fresh
    cilantro (optional)
salt and ground black pepper

1 Heat the oil in a flameproof casserole, add the onion and garlic and sauté for 2–3 minutes, until the onion is softened. Add the cauliflower and sauté, stirring, for another 2–3 minutes until the cauliflower is flecked with brown. Add the cumin seeds and ginger, cook briskly for 1 minute, and then add the tomatoes, ¾ cup water and some salt and pepper.

2 Bring to a boil and then reduce the heat, cover and simmer for 6–7 minutes, until the cauliflower is just tender.

3 Stir in a little lemon juice to sharpen the flavor, if you like, and adjust the seasoning. Scatter with the cilantro, if using, and serve at once.

NUTRITION NOTES	
Per portion:	
Calories	86
Protein	2.5g
Fat	6.2g
Saturated fat	0.9g
Carbohydrate	5.3g
Sugar	4.7g
Fiber (NSP)	1.9g
Calcium	20mg

Roasted Vegetable Salad

Oven roasting brings out all the flavors of these classic Mediterranean vegetables. Serve them hot with broiled or roast meat or fish.

INGREDIENTS

Serves 4
2–3 zucchini
1 Spanish onion
2 red bell peppers
16 cherry tomatoes
2 garlic cloves, chopped
pinch of cumin seed
1 teaspoon fresh thyme or
    4–5 torn basil leaves
¼ cup olive oil
juice of ½ lemon
1–2 teaspoons chili or
    Tabasco sauce
fresh thyme sprigs, to garnish

1 Preheat the oven to 425°F. Trim the zucchini and cut into long strips. Cut the onion into thin wedges, then cut the red peppers into chunks, discarding the seeds and core.

2 Place the vegetables in a roasting pan and, add the tomatoes, garlic, cumin and thyme. Sprinkle with the oil and toss to coat.

3 Cook for 25–30 minutes, until the vegetables are very soft and slightly charred.

4 Blend the lemon juice with the chili or Tabasco sauce and stir into the vegetables. Garnish with thyme and serve.

NUTRITION NOTES	
Per portion:	
Calories	151
Protein	2.8g
Fat	11.8g
Saturated fat	1.7g
Carbohydrate	8.7g
Sugar	7.8g
Fiber (NSP)	2.5g
Calcium	39mg

Red-cooked Tofu with Chinese Mushrooms

Red-cooked is a term applied to Chinese dishes cooked with dark soy sauce. Tamari is a type of soy sauce available in Asian shops that is wheat-free.

INGREDIENTS

Serves 4 as a side dish
8 ounces firm tofu
3 tablespoons tamari
2 tablespoons Chinese rice wine or medium-dry sherry
2 teaspoons dark brown sugar
1 garlic clove, crushed
1 tablespoon grated fresh ginger root
½ teaspoon Chinese five-spice powder
pinch of ground, roasted Szechuan peppercorns
6 dried Chinese black mushrooms
1 teaspoon cornstarch
2 tablespoons vegetable oil
5–6 scallions, white and green parts separated, sliced into 1-inch lengths
small basil leaves, to garnish
rice noodles, to serve

1 Drain the tofu, pat dry with paper towels and cut into 1 inch cubes. Place in a shallow dish.

2 In a small bowl, combine the tamari, rice wine or sherry, sugar, garlic, ginger, five-spice powder and Szechuan peppercorns. Pour the marinade over the tofu, toss well and let marinate for about 30 minutes. Drain, reserving the marinade.

3 Meanwhile, soak the dried black mushrooms in warm water for 20–30 minutes, until soft. Drain, reserving 6 tablespoons of the soaking liquid. Squeeze out any excess liquid from the mushrooms, remove the tough stalks and slice the caps. In a small bowl, blend the cornstarch with the reserved marinade and mushroom soaking liquid.

4 Heat a wok until hot, add the oil and swirl it around to coat the pan. Add the tofu and fry for 2–3 minutes, until evenly golden. Remove from the wok and set aside.

5 Add the mushrooms and white parts of the scallions to the wok and stir-fry for 2 minutes. Pour in the marinade mixture and stir for 1 minute until thickened.

6 Return the tofu to the wok with the scallion greens. Simmer gently for 1–2 minutes. Serve immediately, garnished with basil leaves, on a bed of rice noodles.

— NUTRITION NOTES —	
Per portion:	
Calories	90
Protein	4.5g
Fat	7.9g
Saturated fat	1.1g
Carbohydrate	0.4g
Sugar	0.2g
Fiber (NSP)	0g
Calcium	287mg

Crisp Noodles with Mixed Vegetables

In this dish, rice vermicelli noodles are deep fried until crisp, then tossed into a colorful mixture of stir-fried vegetables.

INGREDIENTS

Serves 3–4
vegetable oil, for deep frying
4 ounces dried vermicelli rice noodles
    or cellophane noodles, broken into
    3-inch lengths
¼ pound yard-long beans or green
    beans, cut into short lengths
1-inch piece fresh ginger, cut into
    shreds
1 fresh red chile, sliced
1½ cups fresh shiitake or button
    mushrooms, thickly sliced
2 large carrots, cut into fine sticks
2 zucchini, cut into fine sticks
a few Chinese cabbage leaves,
    coarsely shredded
1 cup bean sprouts
4 scallions, cut into fine shreds
2 tablespoons tamari
2 tablespoons Chinese rice wine
1 teaspoon sugar
2 tablespoons roughly torn
    cilantro leaves

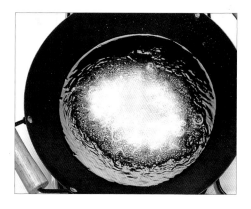

1 Half-fill a wok with oil and heat it to 350°F. Deep fry the raw noodles, a handful at a time, for 1–2 minutes, until puffed and crispy. Drain on paper towels. Carefully pour off all but 2 tablespoons of the oil.

2 Reheat the oil in the wok. When hot, add the beans and stir-fry for 2–3 minutes. Add the ginger, red chile, mushrooms, carrots and zucchini and stir-fry for 1–2 minutes.

3 Add the Chinese cabbage, bean sprouts and scallions to the wok. Stir-fry for 1 minute, then add the tamari, rice wine and sugar. Cook, stirring, for about 30 seconds.

4 Add the noodles and cilantro and toss to mix, taking care not to crush the noodles too much. Serve immediately, piled up on a plate.

COOK'S TIPS

If a milder flavor is preferred, remove the seeds from the chile.

Tamari is a type of soy sauce that is wheat-free. It is available at Asian shops and some health food stores.

NUTRITION NOTES

Per portion:

Calories	184–245
Protein	3.7–4.8g
Fat	6.1–8.16g
Saturated fat	0.9–1.2g
Carbohydrate	27.5–37g
Sugar	3.9–5.2g
Fiber (NSP)	2.2–2.9g
Calcium	41–54mg

DESSERTS AND BAKED GOODS

You do not need to miss out on delicious desserts and baked goods if you are on a restricted diet. The summer fruits in Iced Oranges or Strawberries in Spiced Grape Jelly are impossible to resist. Or try Dutch Apple Cake, which will satisfy even the sweetest tooth. Also in this selection are savory Chive and Potato Scones and Red Lentil Dosas, which make ideal snacks or accompaniments to meat or vegetarian meals.

Pears with Ginger and Star Anise

FREE FROM

Star anise and ginger give a refreshing twist to these poached pears. Serve them chilled.

INGREDIENTS

Serves 4
6 tablespoons sugar
1¼ cups white dessert wine
thinly pared zest and juice of 1 lemon
3-inch piece fresh ginger root, bruised
5 star anise
10 cloves
2½ cups cold water
6 slightly unripe pears
3 tablespoons drained, preserved ginger
   in syrup, sliced
fromage frais, to serve (optional)

1 Place the sugar, dessert wine, lemon zest and juice, fresh ginger, star anise, cloves and water into a saucepan just large enough to hold the pears snugly in an upright position. Bring to a boil.

2 Meanwhile, peel the pears, leaving the stems intact. Add them to the wine mixture, making sure that they are totally immersed in the liquid.

3 Return the wine mixture to a boil, lower the heat, cover and simmer for 15–20 minutes, or until the pears are tender. Lift out the pears with a slotted spoon and place them in a heatproof dish.

4 Boil the wine syrup rapidly until it is reduced by about half, then pour over the pears. Let them cool, then chill.

5 Cut the pears into thick slices and arrange these on four serving plates. Remove the ginger and whole spices from the wine sauce, stir in the sliced preserved ginger and spoon the sauce over the pears. Serve with fromage frais, if desired.

— NUTRITION NOTES —	
Per portion:	
Calories	190
Protein	0.8g
Fat	0.3g
Saturated fat	0g
Carbohydrate	45g
Sugar	44.7g
Fiber (NSP)	5.2g
Calcium	32mg

Spiced Figs with Honey and Orange

Fresh figs, cooked until tender in an orange-flavored honey syrup that is scented with spices.

INGREDIENTS

Serves 6
1⅞ cups fresh orange juice
⅓ cup honey
¼ cup sugar
1 small orange
8 whole cloves
1 pound fresh figs
1 cinnamon stick
mint sprigs or bay leaves, to decorate

1 Put the orange juice, honey and sugar in a heavy saucepan and heat gently until the sugar has dissolved, stirring occasionally.

FREE FROM

2 Stud the orange with the cloves and add to the syrup with the figs and cinnamon. Cover and simmer very gently for 5–10 minutes, until the figs are softened. Transfer to a serving dish and let cool. Serve decorated with mint sprigs or bay leaves.

— NUTRITION NOTES —

Per portion:
Calories	60
Protein	1g
Fat	0.2g
Saturated fat	0g
Carbohydrate	10.3g
Sugar	10.3g
Fiber (NSP)	1.1g
Calcium	31mg

— COOK'S TIP —

Any variety of figs can be used in this recipe, their ripeness determining the cooking time. Choose ones that are plump and firm, and use quickly, as they don't keep well.

Iced Oranges

These pretty little sorbets served in fruit shells originated in beach cafés in the south of France.

INGREDIENTS

Serves 8
⅔ cup sugar
juice of 1 lemon
14 medium oranges
8 fresh bay leaves, to decorate

1 Put the sugar in a heavy pan. Add half the lemon juice, and ½ cup water. Cook over low heat until the sugar has dissolved. Bring to a boil, and boil for 2–3 minutes, until the syrup is clear. Set aside to cool.

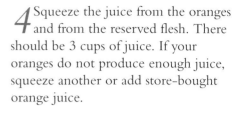

2 Slice the tops off eight of the oranges, to make "hats." Scoop out the flesh of the oranges and reserve in a bowl. Put the empty orange shells and "hats" on a tray and place in the freezer until needed.

3 Grate the zest of the remaining oranges and add to the syrup.

4 Squeeze the juice from the oranges and from the reserved flesh. There should be 3 cups of juice. If your oranges do not produce enough juice, squeeze another or add store-bought orange juice.

5 Stir the orange juice, the remaining lemon juice and 6 tablespoons water into the syrup. Taste, adding more lemon juice or sugar, if desired. Pour the mixture into a shallow freezer container and freeze for 3 hours.

6 Pour the mixture into a bowl and beat thoroughly to break down the ice crystals. Freeze for 4 hours more, until firm, but not solid.

7 Pack the mixture into the orange shells, mounding it up, and set the "hats" on top. Freeze until ready to serve. Just before serving, push a skewer into the tops of the "hats" to make a hole and push in a bay leaf.

NUTRITION NOTES	
Per portion:	
Calories	177
Protein	3g
Fat	0.2g
Saturated fat	0g
Carbohydrate	43.3g
Sugar	43.3g
Fiber (NSP)	4.7g
Calcium	133mg

Black Currant Sorbet

This luscious sorbet is easily made by hand, but it is important to alternately freeze and blend or process the mixture five or six times to get the best result. If you make lots of ice cream and sorbets, it is worth investing in an electric ice-cream maker.

INGREDIENTS

Serves 6

½ cup sugar
2 cups fresh or frozen
   black currants
1 teaspoon lemon juice
2 tablespoons crème de cassis or other
   black currant liqueur (optional)
2 egg whites (optional)

1 Pour 1¼ cups water into a saucepan and add the sugar. Place over a low heat until the sugar has dissolved. Bring to a boil and boil rapidly for 10 minutes, then set the syrup aside to cool.

2 Meanwhile, cook the black currants in a saucepan with 2 tablespoons water over low heat for 5–7 minutes, until tender.

3 Press the cooked black currants and their juice through a sieve placed over a bowl. Stir the resulting black currant purée into the syrup with the lemon juice and the black currant liqueur, if using. Let cool completely, then chill for 1 hour.

4 Pour the chilled black currant syrup into a freezerproof bowl; freeze until slushy, removing and beating occasionally until it reaches this point. Beat the egg whites, if using, in a greasefree bowl until they form soft peaks, then gently fold into the semi-frozen black currant mixture.

5 Freeze the mixture again until firm, then spoon into a food processor or blender and process. Alternately freeze and process or blend until completely smooth. Serve the sorbet straight from the freezer.

NUTRITION NOTES	
Per portion:	
Calories	103
Protein	1.3g
Fat	0g
Saturated fat	0g
Carbohydrate	24.2g
Sugar	24.2g
Fiber (NSP)	1.3g
Calcium	25mg

FREE FROM

Strawberries in Spiced Grape Jelly

What better way to celebrate the strawberry season than with this summer dessert. Raspberries make the perfect alternative if you are allergic to strawberries.

INGREDIENTS

Serves 4

1⅞ cups red grape juice
1 cinnamon stick
1 small orange
1 package powdered gelatin
8 ounces strawberries, chopped
strawberries and shreds of orange zest, to decorate

1 Place the grape juice in a pan with the cinnamon. Thinly pare the zest from the orange and add to the pan. Infuse over very low heat for 10 minutes, then remove the cinnamon and orange zest.

2 Squeeze the juice from the orange and sprinkle the gelatin over the top. Let soften, then stir into the grape juice to dissolve. Let cool until just beginning to set.

3 Stir the strawberries into the setting jelly and quickly pour into a 4-cup mold or serving dish. Chill until set.

4 To turn out, dip the mold quickly into hot water and invert onto a serving plate. Decorate with fresh strawberries and shreds of orange zest.

— NUTRITION NOTES —	
Per portion:	
Calories	85
Protein	1.2g
Fat	0.2g
Saturated fat	0g
Carbohydrate	19.9g
Sugar	19.9g
Fiber (NSP)	1g
Calcium	49mg

Portuguese Rice Pudding

This recipe uses egg yolks that are only very lightly cooked. Omit them, if you wish, and use soy milk in place of cow's milk.

INGREDIENTS

Serves 4–6

6 ounces short-grain rice
2½ cups creamy milk or half-and-half
5 tablespoons butter or margarine
2–3 strips pared lemon zest
½ cup sugar
4 egg yolks (optional)
salt
ground cinnamon, for sprinkling

1 Cook the rice in plenty of lightly salted water for about 5 minutes, so that it is still uncooked but has lost its brittleness.

2 Drain well and then place in a saucepan with the milk, butter or margarine and lemon zest. Very slowly bring to a boil, then cover and simmer, over low heat for about 20 minutes, until the rice is thick and creamy.

3 Turn off the heat and let the rice mixture cool a little. Remove and discard the lemon zest and then stir in the sugar and egg yolks, if using.

4 Divide among 4–6 serving bowls and dust with ground cinnamon. Let cool and serve.

NUTRITION NOTES	
Per portion:	
Calories	378–568
Protein	8–12.1g
Fat	18–27g
Saturated fat	10.2–15.4g
Carbohydrate	47–70g
Sugar	24–37g
Fiber (NSP)	0g
Calcium	154–230mg

FREE FROM

Dutch Apple Cake

The apple topping makes this gluten-free cake really moist and a real treat for those following a special diet.

INGREDIENTS

Makes 8–10 slices

2¼ cups gluten-free self-rising flour
1 teaspoon ground cinnamon
generous ½ cup superfine sugar
4 tablespoons margarine, melted
2 large eggs, beaten
⅔ cup soy milk

For the topping

2 apples
1 tablespoon margarine, melted
2 tablespoons demerara sugar
¼ teaspoon ground cinnamon

1 Preheat the oven to 400°F. Grease and line an 8-inch round cake pan. Sift the flour and cinnamon into a mixing bowl. Stir in the superfine sugar. In a separate bowl, whisk the melted margarine, eggs and milk, then stir into the dry ingredients.

2 Pour into the prepared pan, smooth the surface, then make a shallow hollow around the edge of the mixture.

— NUTRITION NOTES —	
Per portion:	
Calories	220
Protein	4.3g
Fat	5.6g
Saturated fat	1.6g
Carbohydrate	4.1g
Sugar	2.3g
Fiber (NSP)	0.1g
Calcium	110mg

3 Make the topping. Peel and core the apples and slice into thin wedges. Arrange the slices around the hollow of the cake mixture. Brush with melted margarine, then scatter the demerara sugar and ground cinnamon over the top.

4 Bake for 45–50 minutes, or until well risen and golden and a skewer inserted into the center comes out clean. Remove from the pan, peel off the lining paper and serve hot, or cool on a wire rack before slicing.

Pear and Polenta Cake

INGREDIENTS

Makes 10 slices

¾ cup turbinado sugar
4 ripe pears
juice of ½ lemon
2 tablespoons honey
3 eggs
1 teaspoon pure vanilla extract
½ cup sunflower oil
1 cup gluten-free self-rising flour
1 teaspoon gluten-free baking powder
⅓ cup polenta or cornmeal

1 Preheat the oven to 350°F. Grease and line an 8½-inch round cake pan. Scatter 2 tablespoons of the sugar over the bottom of the prepared pan.

2 Peel, core and slice the pears and toss them in the lemon juice. Arrange on the bottom of the cake pan. Drizzle the honey over and set aside.

3 Combine the eggs, vanilla extract and the remaining sugar in a bowl. Beat until thick and creamy, then gradually beat in the oil. Sift together the flour, baking powder and polenta and fold into the egg mixture.

4 Pour the mixture carefully over the pears. Bake for about 50 minutes, or until a skewer inserted into the center comes out clean. Cool in the pan for 10 minutes, then turn the cake out onto a plate and peel off the lining paper. Turn the cake over and serve.

— NUTRITION NOTES —	
Per portion:	
Calories	241
Protein	2.5g
Fat	9.1g
Saturated fat	1.1g
Carbohydrate	39.3g
Sugar	27.2g
Fiber (NSP)	1.75g
Calcium	50.5mg

Oatcakes

These oatcakes are delicious served as a snack with grapes and wedges of cheese. They are also good topped with honey for breakfast.

INGREDIENTS

Makes 8
1 cup oatmeal, plus extra for sprinkling
½ teaspoon salt
pinch of baking soda
1 tablespoon margarine
5 tablespoons water

— COOK'S TIP —

To achieve a neat round, place a 10-inch plate on top of the oatcake dough. Cut away any excess dough with a spatula, then remove the plate.

1 Preheat the oven to 300°F. Mix the oatmeal with the salt and baking soda in a large mixing bowl.

2 Melt the margarine with the water in a small saucepan. Bring to a boil, then add to the oatmeal mixture and mix to a moist dough.

3 Turn the dough onto a surface sprinkled with extra oatmeal and knead to a smooth ball. Turn a large baking sheet upside-down, grease it, sprinkle it lightly with oatmeal and place the ball of dough on top. Sprinkle the dough with oatmeal, then roll out to a 10-inch round.

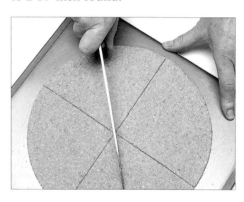

4 Cut the round into eight sections, ease them apart slightly and bake for 50–60 minutes, until crisp.

5 Let cool on the baking sheet, then carefully remove the oatcakes with a spatula.

— NUTRITION NOTES —

Per portion:
Calories	101
Protein	2.7g
Fat	3.4g
Saturated fat	0.7g
Carbohydrate	15.9g
Sugar	0g
Fiber (NSP)	1.5g
Calcium	12mg

Chive and Potato Scones

These little scones make an ideal breakfast treat for those following a wheat- or gluten-free diet.

INGREDIENTS

Makes 20

1 pound potatoes, peeled and cut
   into chunks
1 cup plain gluten-free
   flour, sifted
3 tablespoons olive oil
2 tablespoons snipped chives
vegetable oil, for greasing
salt and ground black pepper
broiled bacon and tomatoes, to serve

— VARIATION —

If you are not following a gluten—or wheat-free diet, use all-purpose flour.

1 Cook the potatoes in a saucepan of boiling salted water for 15 minutes, or until tender, then drain thoroughly. Return the potatoes to the clean pan and mash them.

— NUTRITION NOTES —

Per portion:

Calories	50
Protein	1.1g
Fat	1.7g
Saturated fat	0.2g
Carbohydrate	8.3g
Sugar	0.4g
Fiber (NSP)	0.5g
Calcium	9.2mg

2 Add the flour, olive oil and snipped chives with a little salt and pepper to the hot mashed potato in the pan. Mix to a soft dough.

3 Roll out the dough on a surface dusted with gluten-free flour to a thickness of ¼-inch; cut out rounds with a 2-inch pastry cutter.

4 Lightly grease, then heat a griddle or frying pan. Place the potato rounds on the hot griddle or frying pan. Cook over low heat, in batches if necessary, for about 10 minutes, turning once, until the scones are golden brown on both sides. Serve hot with broiled bacon slices and tomatoes.

Red Lentil Dosas

Dosas are southern Indian breads. They are very different from traditional north Indian breads, such as chapatis, as they are made from lentils and rice rather than flour, so they are the perfect choice for people who have a gluten or wheat allergy. *Dosas* are like pancakes and are delicious freshly cooked for breakfast, or as an accompaniment to main dishes, especially stews, curries and rice dishes.

INGREDIENTS

Makes 6 dosas

¾ cup long-grain rice
¼ cup red lentils
1 teaspoon salt
½ teaspoon ground turmeric
½ teaspoon ground black pepper
2 tablespoons chopped cilantro
oil, for frying and drizzling

1 Place the rice and lentils in a bowl, cover with 1 cup warm water and let soak for 8 hours, then drain off the water and reserve. Place the rice and lentils in a food processor and blend until smooth. Blend in the reserved water.

3 Stir in the salt, turmeric, pepper and cilantro. Heat a heavy frying pan over a medium heat for a few minutes until hot. Smear with a little oil and add about 2–3 tablespoons of the batter.

4 Using the rounded bottom of a soup spoon, gently spread the batter out, using a circular motion, to make a 6-inch diameter *dosa*.

5 Cook for 1½–2 minutes, or until set. Drizzle a little oil over the *dosa* and around the edges. Turn over and cook for about 1 minute or until golden. Keep warm in a low oven or over simmering water while cooking the remaining *dosas*. Serve warm.

2 Transfer to a bowl, cover with plastic wrap and set aside in a warm place to ferment for about 24 hours.

VARIATION

To make spicy coconut *dosas*, add 1/4 cup grated coconut, 1 tablespoon grated fresh ginger and 1 finely chopped chile to the batter just before cooking.

NUTRITION NOTES

Per portion:

Calories	138
Protein	3.8g
Fat	2.8g
Saturated fat	0.5g
Carbohydrate	26.1g
Sugar	0.2g
Fiber (NSP)	0.5g
Calcium	17mg

INFORMATION FILE

USEFUL ADDRESSES

Always Natural Foods
3323 East Patterson Road
Beaver Valley Shopping Center
Bearvercreek, OH 45430
Tel: (937) 426-7772
Fax: (937) 426-7464

The American Academy of Allergies, Asthma and Immunology
611 East Wells Street
Milwaukee, WI 53202
Tel: (800) 822-2762

The American Dietetic Association
216 West Jackson Boulevard
Chicago, IL 60606
Tel: (312) 899-0040
Fax: (800) 366-1655

American Society for Nutritional Sciences
9650 Rockville Pike
Bethesda, MD 20814
Tel: (301) 530-7050
Fax: (301) 571-1892

Authentic Foods
1850 West 169th Street
Suite B
Gardena, CA 90247
Tel: (800) 806-4737
Fax: (310) 366-6938

Beta Pure Foods
Morr Pure Foods, Inc.
335 Spreckels Drive
Suite D
Aptos, CA 95003
Tel: (408) 685-6565
Fax: (408) 685-6569
www.betapure.com

Better Health USA, Inc.
1620 West Oakland Park Boulevard
Suite 401
Fort Lauderdale, FL 33311
Tel: (800) 684-2231
Fax: (954) 739-2780

The Celiac Group
1269 Third Avenue
San Francisco, CA 94122
Tel/Fax: (415) 664-3820

Center for Food Safety & Applied Nutrition
200 C Street SW
Washington, DC 20204
www.cfsan.fda.gov

Clearwater Natural Foods
11 Housatonic Street
Lenox, MA 01240
Tel: (413) 637-2721

Dietary Specialties Inc.
P.O. Box 227
Rochester, NY 14601-0227
Tel: (800) 544-0099

Earth Fare
Rockwood Plaza
213 Oak Street
Forest City, NC 28043
Tel: (828) 245-6578
Fax: (828) 245-6625

Ener-G Foods
P.O. Box 84487
Seattle, WA 98124-5787
Tel: (800) 331-5222

The Food Allergy Network
10400 Eaton Place
Suite 107
Fairfax, VA 22030-2208
Tel: (800) 929-4040
Fax: (703) 691-2713

Food and Nutrition Information Center
National Agricultural Library
Room 304
10301 Baltimore Avenue
Beltsville, MD 20705-2351
Tel: (301) 504-5719

Galaxy Foods Company
2441 Viscount Row
Orlando, FL 32809
Tel: (800) 808-2325

Gifts of Nature, Inc.
P.O. Box 309
Corvalis, MT 59828
Tel: (406) 375-9429
Fax: (406) 375-0013

The Gluten-Free Pantry
P.O. Box 840
Glastonbury, CT 06033
Tel: (800) 291-8386
Fax: (800) 633-6853

Miss Roben's Inc.
P.O. Box 1434
Frederick, MD 21702
Tel: (800) 891-0083
Fax: (301) 665-9584

Nancy's Natural Foods
266 NW First Avenue
Canby, OR 97013
Tel: (877) 862-4457

Summercorn Foods
1410 Cato Springs Road
Fayetteville, AR 72701
Tel: (888) 328-9473
Fax: (501) 443-5771

Vegan Action
P.O. Box 4353
Berkeley, CA 94704
Tel: (510) 548-5377

INDEX

Additives, 16-17, 21
Allergies, 6-7
    additives, 16-17
    cereal foods, 10-11
    in children, 21
    diagnosing, 17
    diet testing, 18–19
    milk and dairy products, 12–13
    other problem foods, 14–15
Anaphylactic shock, 14
Apple cake, Dutch, 90
Apricots: lamb tagine, 42
Arugula and cilantro salad, 38

Beef rolls with garlic and tomato
    sauce, 49
Black and orange salad, 38
Black currant sorbet, 87
Bread, 8
    red lentil dosas, 94
Buckwheat noodles with smoked
    trout, 66

Cabbage parcels, pork-stuffed, 47
Cakes: Dutch apple cake, 90
    pear and polenta cake, 90
Calcium, 13
Cauliflower with tomatoes and
    cumin, 78
Cereals, 8, 10–11
Cheese: Greek salad, 36
Chicken: Mediterranean roasted, 52
    stoved chicken, 54
    with forty cloves of garlic, 50
Children: cooking for, 21
    hyperactivity, 17
Chili dip, spicy potato wedges
    with, 30
Chive and potato scones, 93
Coconut, spiced shrimp with, 67
Coeliac disease, 10, 11
Cilantro, arugula salad and, 38
Corn (maize) intolerance, 11
Dairy foods, 8–9, 12–13
Desensitization, 17
Desserts, 83–9
Diet testing, 18–19

Dosas, red lentil, 94
Duck with pears, spiced, 55
Dutch apple cake, 90

Eggplant: ratatouille, 72
    spiced eggplant salad, 36
Eggs, 15, 21
Elimination diets, 17, 19
Exclusion diets, 17, 18–19

Fasting, 19
Fava beans: lamb casserole
    with garlic and, 45
    fava bean dip, 32
Figs with honey and orange, 85
Fish and shellfish, 9, 14, 57–67
    fish balls with Chinese greens, 60
    fish with spinach and lime, 59
    halibut with tomato vinaigrette, 64
    Mediterranean baked fish, 58
    red snapper with cumin, 62
    spicy fish brochettes, 62
    tuna with pan-fried tomatoes, 61
Food diary, 19
Fruit, 8

Garlic: chicken with forty cloves of
    garlic, 50
Globe artichokes, green beans and
    garlic dressing, 31
Gluten, 10–11
Grapefruit cocktail, melon and, 28
Grape leaves, stuffed, 74
Greek salad, 36
Green beans with tomatoes, 76
Green peppercorn-and cinnamon-
    crusted lamb, 44

Halibut with tomato vinaigrette, 64
Ham: prosciutto with mango, 28
Hyperactivity, 17

Jelly: strawberries in spiced grape
    jelly, 88

Lactose intolerance, 12–13
Lamb: green peppercorn-and
    cinnamon-crusted lamb, 44
    lamb casserole with garlic and
    fava beans, 45
    lamb pie with mustard-potato
    crust, 43
    lamb tagine, 42
    Turkish lamb pilaf, 46
Lentils: lentil soup with tomatoes, 24
    red lentil dosas, 94

Mango, prosciutto with, 28
Meat and poultry, 9, 41–55

Mediterranean baked fish, 58
Mediterranean roasted chicken, 52
Melon and grapefruit cocktail, 28
Middle Eastern vegetable stew, 71
Milk allergy, 12–13, 21
Mushrooms: polenta with
    mushroom sauce, 77
    red-cooked tofu with Chinese
    mushrooms, 80

Noodles: buckwheat noodles with
    smoked trout, 66
    crisp noodles with mixed
    vegetables, 81
Nuts, 14

Oatcakes, 92
Olives: black and orange salad, 38
    with spicy marinades, 32
Oranges: black and orange salad, 38
    iced oranges, 86
    pork tenderloin with sage and, 48
Organic foods, 9

Pears: spiced duck with, 55
    with ginger and star anise, 84
Peppers: Spanish rice salad, 34
Pilaf, Turkish lamb, 46
Polenta: pear and polenta cake, 90
    with mushroom sauce, 77
Pork: pork tenderloin with sage and
    orange, 48
    pork-stuffed cabbage parcels, 47
Portuguese rice pudding, 89
Potatoes, 8
    chive and potato scones, 93
    lamb pie with mustard-potato
    crust, 43
    salad Niçoise, 35
    spicy wedges with chili dip, 30
    stoved chicken, 54
Poultry and meat, 41–55
Poussins, spiced grilled, 50
Prosciutto with mango, 28
Pumpkin soup, 26

Rare foods diet, 19
RAST test, 17
Ratatouille, 72
Red-cooked tofu with Chinese
    mushrooms, 80
Red lentil dosas, 94
Red snapper with cumin, 62
Restaurants, 20
Rice: Portuguese rice pudding, 89
    red lentil dosas, 94
    risotto with spring vegetables, 73
    Spanish rice salad, 34
    spinach and rice soup, 24

stuffed grape leaves, 74
Turkish lamb pilaf, 46

Salads: black and orange, 38
    arugula and cilantro, 38
    Greek salad, 36
    roasted vegetable, 78
    salad Niçoise, 35
    Spanish rice, 34
    spiced eggplant, 36
Scones, chive and potato, 93
Shrimp with coconut, spiced, 67
Skin prick test, 17
Smoked trout, buckwheat noodles
    with, 66
Sorbets: black currant sorbet, 87
    iced oranges, 86
Soups, 24–7
Soy products, 15
Spanish rice salad, 34
Spinach: fish with lime and, 59
    spinach and rice soup, 24
Stoved chicken, 54
Strawberries in spiced grape jelly, 88
Summer tomato soup, 26
Summer vegetables, braised, 70

Tofu: red-cooked tofu with
    Chinese mushrooms, 80
Tomatoes: cauliflower with cumin
    and, 78
    fresh tuna and tomato stew, 65
    Greek salad, 36
    green beans with, 76
    halibut with tomato vinaigrette, 64
    lentil soup with, 24
    ratatouille, 72
    spicy potato wedges with chili
    dip, 30
    summer tomato soup, 26
    tuna with pan-fried tomatoes, 61
Tuna: fresh tuna and tomato stew, 65
    salad Niçoise, 35
    with pan-fried tomatoes, 61
Turkish lamb pilaf, 46

Vegetables, 8, 69-81
    braised summer vegetables, 70
    crisp noodles with mixed
    vegetables, 81
    Middle Eastern vegetable stew, 71
    ratatouille, 72
    risotto with spring vegetables, 73
    roasted vegetable salad, 78

Wheat allergy, 10, 11, 21

Yeast, 15